W9-AWC-449

FAVORITE BRAND NAME

BEST LOVED

APPETIZERS

Publications International, Ltd.

Favorite Brand Name Recipes at www.fbnr.com

Copyright © 2002 Publications International, Ltd.

All rights reserved. This publication may not be reproduced or quoted in whole or in part by any means whatsoever without written permission from:

Louis Weber, CEO
Publications International, Ltd.
7373 North Cicero Avenue
Lincolnwood, Illinois 60712

Permission is never granted for commercial purposes.

All recipes and photographs that contain specific brand names are copyrighted by those companies and/or associations, unless otherwise specified. All photographs *except* those on pages 65, 191 and 351 copyright © Publications International, Ltd.

DOLE® is a registered trademark of Dole Food Company, Inc.

Ortega is a registered trademark of Nestlé.

TACO BELL® and HOME ORIGINALS® are trademarks owned and licensed by Taco Bell Corp.

Some of the products listed in this publication may be in limited distribution.

Photography on pages 45, 55, 89, 155, 173, 181, 189, 219, 225, 259, 267 and 303 by Proffitt Photography Ltd., Chicago.
Photographer: Laurie Proffitt
Prop Stylist: Paula Walters
Food Stylist: Carol Smoler
Food Stylist's Assistant: Vanessa DuBiel
Photographer's Assistant: Sarah Gilbert

Pictured on the front cover *(clockwise from top left):* Artichoke Frittata *(page 55),* Festive Taco Cups *(page 154),* Ortega® Green Chile Guacamole *(page 179)* and Spanish-Style Garlic Shrimp *(page 238).*

ISBN: 0-7853-6263-0

Library of Congress Catalog Card Number: 2002100178

Manufactured in China.

8 7 6 5 4 3 2 1

Microwave Cooking: Microwave ovens vary in wattage. Use the cooking times as guidelines and check for doneness before adding more time.

Preparation/Cooking Times: Preparation times are based on the approximate amount of time required to assemble the recipe before cooking, baking, chilling or serving. These times include preparation steps such as measuring, chopping and mixing. The fact that some preparations and cooking can be done simultaneously is taken into account. Preparation of optional ingredients and serving suggestions is not included.

Contents

✿ ✿ ✿

Dips & Spreads

Roasted Red Pepper Spread

1 cup roasted red peppers, rinsed and drained

1 package (8 ounces) cream cheese, softened

1 packet (1 ounce) HIDDEN VALLEY® Original Ranch® Salad Dressing & Recipe Mix

Baguette slices and sliced ripe olives (optional)

Blot dry red peppers. In a food processor fitted with a metal blade, combine peppers, cream cheese and salad dressing & recipe mix; process until smooth. Spread on baguette slices and garnish with olives, if desired.

Makes 2 cups

Roasted Red Pepper Spread

Cheddar Cheese and Rice Roll

Prep Time: 20 minutes   **Cook Time:** none

2 cups cooked UNCLE BEN'S®
ORIGINAL CONVERTED®
Brand Rice

3 cups grated low-fat
Cheddar cheese

¾ cup fat-free cream cheese,
softened

1 can (4½ ounces) green
chilies, drained, chopped

⅛ teaspoon hot sauce

1½ cups chopped walnuts

PREP: CLEAN: Wash hands. Combine rice, Cheddar cheese, cream cheese, chilies and hot sauce. Mix by hand or in food processor. Shape mixture into a log. Roll in walnuts. Wrap tightly with plastic wrap and refrigerate 1 hour.

SERVE: Serve with assorted crackers.

CHILL: Refrigerate leftovers immediately.   *Makes 15 servings*

Onion Chip Dip

Prep Time: 5 minutes   **Microwave Time:** 5 minutes

1 pound (16 ounces)
VELVEETA® Pasteurized
Prepared Cheese
Product, cut up

1 container (8 ounces)
BREAKSTONE'S® or
KNUDSEN® Sour Cream

2 tablespoons chopped green
onion

1. Microwave Velveeta in 1½-quart microwavable bowl on HIGH 4 minutes or until melted, stirring after 2 minutes.

2. Stir in sour cream and onion. Microwave 1 minute. Serve hot with potato chips.   *Makes 2¾ cups*

Cheddar Cheese and Rice Roll

Hot Artichoke and Tuna Spread

Prep Time: 35 minutes

1 (3-ounce) pouch of STARKIST® Solid White or Chunk Light Tuna, drained

1 jar (12 ounces) marinated artichoke hearts, drained

1 to 2 cloves garlic

1 cup shredded mozzarella cheese

½ cup grated Parmesan cheese

¼ cup chopped canned green chilies

1 tablespoon minced green onion

2 to 3 tablespoons mayonnaise

Hot pepper sauce to taste

French bread or assorted crackers

In food processor bowl with metal blade, place all ingredients except bread. Process until well blended but not puréed. Transfer mixture to ovenproof serving dish. Bake, uncovered, in 350°F oven about 30 minutes or until mixture is golden. Serve hot with French bread.

Makes 12 servings

Note: This mixture may be baked in small hollowed bread shell. Wrap in foil; bake as above. Open top of foil last 5 minutes of baking.

Tip: Mixture keeps well, tightly covered, in refrigerator for up to 5 days.

Easy Cheese Fondue

1 pound low-sodium Swiss cheese (Gruyére, Emmentaler or combination of both), divided

2 tablespoons cornstarch

1 garlic clove, crushed

1 cup HOLLAND HOUSE® White or White with Lemon Cooking Wine

1 tablespoon kirsch or cherry brandy (optional)

Pinch nutmeg

Ground black pepper

1. In medium bowl, coat cheese with cornstarch; set aside. Rub inside of ceramic fondue pot or heavy saucepan with garlic; discard garlic. Bring wine to gentle simmer over medium heat. Gradually stir in cheese to ensure smooth fondue. Once smooth, stir in brandy, if desired. Garnish with nutmeg and pepper.

2. Serve with bite-sized chunks of French bread, broccoli, cauliflower, tart apples or pears. Spear with fondue forks or wooden skewers.

Makes 1¼ cups

Helpful Hint

Gruyère and Emmentaler cheeses are both made from cow's milk and have a rich, sweet nutty flavor. These cheeses are widely available in supermarkets and cheese shops; they are used for cooking as well as eating with bread, crackers, fruit, etc.

Hidden Valley® Salsa Ranch Dip

1 container (16 ounces) sour cream (2 cups)

1 packet (1 ounce) HIDDEN VALLEY® Original Ranch® Dips Mix

½ cup thick and chunky salsa

Chopped tomatoes and diced green chiles (optional)

Tortilla chips, for dipping

Combine sour cream and dips mix. Stir in salsa. Add tomatoes and chiles, if desired. Chill 1 hour. Serve with tortilla chips.

Makes 2½ cups

Curried Fruit Dip

Prep Time: 10 minutes

1 cup sour cream

3 tablespoons mango chutney

2 tablespoons unsweetened pineapple juice

2 teaspoons honey Dijon mustard

1 teaspoon curry powder

1 teaspoon grated orange peel

Assorted cut-up fresh fruit and vegetables

1. Place sour cream in small bowl. Stir in chutney, pineapple juice, mustard, curry and orange peel until well blended.

2. Transfer dip to serving bowl. Serve immediately with fresh fruit and vegetables or cover with plastic wrap and refrigerate until ready to serve.

Makes 1½ cups

Note: Curry powder is a blend of up to 20 ground spices, herbs and seeds. It should be stored in an airtight container to preserve its pungency.

Hidden Valley® Salsa Ranch Dip

Garlic Bean Dip

Prep Time: 10 minutes

4 cloves garlic

1 can (15½ ounces) pinto or black beans, rinsed and drained

¼ cup pimiento-stuffed green olives

4½ teaspoons lemon juice

½ teaspoon ground cumin

Assorted fresh vegetables and crackers

Place garlic in food processor; process until minced. Add beans, olives, lemon juice and cumin; process until well blended but not entirely smooth. Serve with vegetables and crackers.

Makes about 1½ cups

Note: The spice cumin is widely used in Middle Eastern, Asian and Mediterranean cooking. It is available in seed and ground form and adds a nutty flavor to dishes.

Tip: To save time, buy fresh vegetables, such as carrots and celery, already cut up from the produce section of the supermarket.

Helpful Hint

Pinto beans are reddish-brown beans grown in the American Southwest and commonly used in making refried beans and chili. Pink beans can be subsituted for pinto beans—they are lighter in color before cooking but look the same afterwards.

Garlic Bean Dip

Nutty Cheese Crock

Preparation Time: 15 minutes   **Total Time:** 15 minutes

1 cup shredded Cheddar
   cheese (4 ounces)

¾ cup margarine or butter,
   softened

½ cup grated Parmesan
   cheese

¼ cup GREY POUPON® Dijon
   Mustard

¼ cup PLANTERS® Walnuts,
   chopped

2 cloves garlic, crushed

Herbed Pita Crisps (recipe
   follows) or RITZ® Crackers

1. Blend all ingredients except Herbed Pita Crisps in medium bowl with mixer. Refrigerate until serving time.

2. Let stand 10 minutes at room temperature before serving. Serve as a spread on Herbed Pita Crisps or crackers.   *Makes 2¾ cups*

Herbed Pita Crisps

1 (12-ounce) package pita bread (6-inch rounds)

½ cup margarine or butter

2 cloves garlic, minced

1 teaspoon minced fresh thyme leaves or ⅓ teaspoon dried thyme leaves

1 teaspoon minced fresh oregano or ⅓ teaspoon dried oregano leaves

1. Split each pita bread into 2 rounds. Blend margarine or butter, garlic and herbs in small bowl. Spread herbed mixture on pita rounds; cut each round into 8 wedges.

2. Bake in preheated 350°F oven for 8 to 10 minutes or until golden brown.   *Makes 8 dozen*

Nutty Cheese Crock

Three Mushroom Ratatouille

1 package (3½ ounces) fresh shiitake mushrooms*

1 tablespoon olive oil

1 large onion, chopped

4 cloves garlic, minced

1 package (8 ounces) button mushrooms, chopped

1 package (6 ounces) crimini mushrooms, chopped

1 cup chicken broth

½ cup chopped fresh tomato

2 tablespoons chopped fresh parsley

2 tablespoons grated Parmesan cheese

3 pita breads (6 inches each)

Italian parsley for garnish

*Or, substitute 1 ounce dried black Chinese mushrooms. Place dried mushrooms in small bowl; cover with warm water. Soak 20 minutes to soften. Drain; squeeze out excess moisture. Prepare as directed in Step 1.

1. Remove stems from shiitake mushrooms; discard stems and chop caps.

2. Preheat broiler. Heat oil in large skillet over medium heat until hot. Add onion and garlic. Cook 5 minutes, stirring occasionally. Add all chopped mushrooms; cook 5 minutes more, stirring often.

3. Add chicken broth; bring to a boil. Cook about 10 minutes or until liquid is absorbed. Remove from heat. Stir in tomato, chopped parsley and cheese. Spoon into bowl.

4. Meanwhile, split each pita bread horizontally in half. Stack halves; cut stack into 6 wedges. Arrange wedges in single layer on baking sheet. Broil 4 inches from heat 1 to 3 minutes or until wedges are toasted.

5. Arrange toasted pita bread triangles and warm dip in basket. Garnish, if desired.

Makes about 2¼ cups

Smoky Eggplant Dip

Prep Time: 30 minutes   **Cook Time:** 20 minutes   **Chill Time:** 30 minutes

1 large eggplant (about
    1 pound)

¼ cup olive oil

3 tablespoons *Frank's®*
    RedHot® Cayenne Pepper
    Sauce

2 tablespoons peanut butter
    or tahini paste

1 tablespoon lemon juice

2 cloves garlic, minced

¾ teaspoon salt

½ teaspoon ground cumin

Spicy Pita Chips (recipe
    follows)

1. Prepare grill. Place eggplant on oiled grid. Grill, over hot coals, 15 minutes or until soft and skin is charred, turning often. Remove from grill; cool until easy enough to handle.

2. Peel skin from eggplant with paring knife; discard. Coarsely chop eggplant. Place in strainer or kitchen towel. Press out excess liquid.

3. Place eggplant in food processor; add oil, *RedHot* Sauce, peanut butter, lemon juice, garlic, salt and cumin. Cover; process until mixture is very smooth. Spread eggplant mixture on serving platter. Cover; refrigerate until chilled. Serve with Spicy Pita Chips.
Makes 1½ cups dip

Spicy Pita Chips: Split 4 pita bread rounds in half lengthwise. Combine ½ cup olive oil, ¼ cup *Frank's RedHot* and 1 tablespoon minced garlic in small bowl. Brush mixture on both sides of pitas. Place pitas on grid. Grill, over medium coals, about 5 minutes or until crispy, turning once. Cut pitas into triangles.

Seafood Spread

1 package (8 ounces) cream cheese, softened

½ pound smoked whitefish, skinned, boned, flaked

2 tablespoons minced green onion

1 tablespoon plus
   1 teaspoon chopped fresh dill

1 teaspoon lemon juice

¼ teaspoon black pepper

Rye bread slices or assorted crackers

Beat cream cheese in medium bowl with electric mixer on medium speed until smooth. Add remaining ingredients except bread, mixing until blended. Refrigerate until ready to serve.

Serve with rye bread slices or assorted crackers. Garnish with lime wedges, if desired.

Makes 1½ cups (12 servings)

Warm Broccoli 'n Cheddar Dip

1 envelope LIPTON® RECIPE SECRETS® Onion or Savory Herb with Garlic Soup Mix*

1 container (16 ounces) sour cream

1 package (10 ounces) frozen chopped broccoli or spinach, thawed and squeezed dry

1 cup shredded Cheddar cheese (about 4 ounces)

1. Preheat oven to 350°F. In 1-quart casserole, combine soup mix, sour cream, broccoli and ¾ cup cheese. Sprinkle with remaining ¼ cup cheese.

2. Bake uncovered 30 minutes or until heated through.

3. Serve with your favorite dippers.

Makes 3 cups dip

Seafood Spread

Mike's Sensational Salsa

2 cans (14.5 ounces) HUNT'S® Choice-Cut Diced Tomatoes, one can drained

¼ cup sliced green onion (including white and green portions)

3 tablespoons chopped onion

2 tablespoons chopped fresh cilantro

1 tablespoon diced green chiles

2 teaspoons diced jalapeños (canned or fresh), seeds included

1 ½ teaspoons sugar

1 teaspoon minced fresh garlic

¼ teaspoon salt

¼ teaspoon cumin

¼ teaspoon hot pepper sauce

Baked tortilla chips *or* fresh cut vegetables

1. In medium bowl, combine Hunt's Choice-Cut Diced Tomatoes and *remaining* ingredients *except* chips or vegetables.

2. Cover and refrigerate at least 2 hours or overnight.

3. Remove 30 minutes before serving.

4. Stir once before serving. Serve with chips or vegetables.

Makes 12 (¼ -cup) servings

Helpful Hint

Look for green onions with a firm white base and crisp bright green tops. Store them in a plastic bag in the vegetable crisper in the refrigerator for up to 5 days.

Spectacular Shrimp Spread

½ pound cooked deveined peeled Florida rock shrimp

1 can (13 ounces) artichoke hearts, drained

1 cup mayonnaise*

½ cup shredded Parmesan cheese

¼ teaspoon ground lemon pepper

⅛ teaspoon salt

Dash cayenne pepper

*May substitute ½ cup mayonnaise and ½ cup plain yogurt for mayonnaise.

Preheat oven to 400°F. Finely chop rock shrimp and artichoke hearts; place in medium bowl. Add mayonnaise, cheese, lemon pepper, salt and cayenne pepper; mix well. Spoon shrimp mixture into 9-inch pie pan or 1-quart shallow baking dish. Bake 10 minutes or until hot and bubbly. Serve hot with crackers, if desired.

Makes about 3¾ cups

*Favorite recipe from **Florida Department of Agriculture and Consumer Services, Bureau of Seafood and Aquaculture***

Cheddar Beer Dip

Preparation Time: 15 minutes   **Total Time:** 15 minutes

1 (8-ounce) package PHILADELPHIA® Cream Cheese, softened

½ cup beer

2 cups KRAFT® Shredded Cheddar Cheese (8 ounces)

WHEAT THINS® Snack Crackers

1. Beat cream cheese in medium bowl with electric mixer until smooth; gradually blend in beer. Add Cheddar cheese, beating until well blended.

2. Refrigerate until serving time. Serve as dip with snack crackers.

Makes about 2½ cups

Pesto Brie

2 tablespoons GREY
POUPON® Dijon Mustard

2 tablespoons prepared
pesto sauce

1 (8-ounce) wheel Brie
cheese

2 tablespoons PLANTERS®
Walnuts, finely chopped

Chopped tomatoes and
fresh basil leaves, for
garnish

Assorted NABISCO®
Crackers or STELLA
D'ORO® Breadsticks

Blend mustard and pesto in small bowl; set aside. Cut cheese in half horizontally. Place bottom half on greased baking sheet, cut-side up; spread with half the pesto mixture. Replace top of Brie, cut-side down; spread with remaining pesto mixture and sprinkle with nuts.

Bake at 350°F for 3 to 4 minutes or until cheese is slightly softened. Do not overbake. Transfer to serving dish. Garnish with chopped tomatoes and basil leaves. Serve with assorted crackers or breadsticks.
Makes 6 to 8 appetizer servings

Lawry's® Fiesta Dip

1 package (1 ounce)
LAWRY'S® Taco Spices
& Seasonings

1 pint (16 ounces) sour
cream

In medium bowl, combine ingredients. Mix well. Refrigerate until ready to serve.
Makes 2 cups

Serving Suggestion: Serve with chips and crackers.

Hint: Dip may be served with tortilla chips and fresh cut vegetables such as carrots, broccoli, cauliflower and zucchini.

Pesto Brie

Hot French Onion Dip

1 envelope LIPTON® RECIPE SECRETS® Onion Soup Mix

1 container (16 ounces) sour cream

2 cups shredded Swiss cheese (about 8 ounces)

¼ cup HELLMAN'S® or BEST FOODS® Mayonnaise

1. Preheat oven to 375°F. In 1-quart casserole, combine soup mix, sour cream, 1¾ cups Swiss cheese and mayonnaise.

2. Bake uncovered 20 minutes or until heated through. Sprinkle with remaining ¼ cup cheese.

3. Serve, if desired, with sliced French bread or your favorite dippers.

Makes 2 cups dip

Pineapple-Mango Salsa

Prep Time: 15 minutes   **Chill Time:** 30 minutes

1 ½ cups DOLE® Fresh Pineapple Chunks

1 ripe DOLE® Mango, peeled and chopped

½ cup chopped red cabbage

⅓ cup finely chopped DOLE® Red Onion

¼ cup chopped fresh cilantro

2 tablespoons lime juice

1 to 2 serrano or jalapeño chiles, seeded and minced

- Stir together pineapple, mango, cabbage, red onion, cilantro, lime juice and chiles in medium bowl. Cover and chill for at least 30 minutes to blend flavors. Serve salsa over grilled chicken with grilled vegetables. Garnish with lime wedges, if desired.

- Salsa can also be served as a dip with tortilla chips or spooned over quesadillas or tacos.

Makes 3½ cups

Hot French Onion Dip

Deviled Vegetable Crab Spread

Preparation Time: 30 minutes   **Cook Time:** 20 minutes   **Total Time:** 50 minutes

1 (8-ounce) package
   PHILADELPHIA® Cream
   Cheese, softened

¼ cup GREY POUPON® Dijon
   Mustard

2 tablespoons milk

12 PREMIUM® Crackers (any
   variety), finely crushed
   (½ cup crumbs)

1 (6-ounce) can crabmeat or
   tuna, drained and flaked

¼ cup chopped green onions

¼ cup chopped red bell
   pepper

   Additional PREMIUM®
   Crackers

1. Beat cream cheese in small bowl with electric mixer at medium speed until smooth; add mustard and milk, beating until well blended.

2. Add cracker crumbs, crabmeat or tuna, green onions and bell pepper. Place in greased 8-inch pie plate or small baking dish.

3. Bake at 350°F for 20 minutes or until golden brown and hot. Serve as a spread with crackers. *Makes about 2⅓ cups*

Helpful Hint

Make sure to pick over crabmeat with your fingers before using it. Occasionally you'll find tiny pieces of shell that need to be removed.

Black Bean Salsa

1 can (14½ ounces) black
  beans, rinsed and
  drained
1 cup frozen corn, thawed
1 large tomato, chopped
¼ cup chopped green onions
2 tablespoons chopped fresh
  cilantro
2 tablespoons lemon juice
1 tablespoon vegetable oil
1 teaspoon chili powder
¼ teaspoon salt
6 corn tortillas

1. Combine beans, corn, tomato, green onions, cilantro, lemon
   juice, oil, chili powder and salt in medium bowl; mix well.

2. Preheat oven to 400°F. Cut each tortilla into 8 wedges; place on
   ungreased baking sheet. Bake 6 to 8 minutes or until edges begin
   to brown. Serve tortilla wedges warm or at room temperature
   with salsa. Garnish with lemon wedges and additional fresh
   cilantro, if desired.   *Makes 6 servings*

Sour Cream 'N Bacon Dip

Prep Time: 5 minutes   **Microwave Time:** 5 minutes

1 pound (16 ounces)
  VELVEETA® Pasteurized
  Prepared Cheese
  Product, cut up
1 container (8 ounces)
  BREAKSTONE'S® or
  KNUDSEN® Sour Cream
2 tablespoons OSCAR
  MAYER® Real Bacon Bits

1. Microwave Velveeta in 1½-quart microwavable bowl on HIGH
   4 minutes or until melted, stirring after 2 minutes.

2. Stir in sour cream and bacon bits. Microwave 1 minute. Serve hot
   with potato chips.   *Makes 2½ cups*

Make-Ahead Directions: Velveeta dips can travel to any party.
Simply assemble ingredients at home in a zipper-style plastic bag
and tote. At the party, transfer ingredients into microwavable bowl
and heat according to recipe directions.

Herbed Blue Cheese Spread with Garlic Toasts

1 ⅓ cups 1% low-fat cottage cheese

1 ¼ cups (5 ounces) crumbled blue, feta or goat cheese

1 large clove garlic

2 teaspoons lemon juice

2 green onions with tops, sliced (about ¼ cup)

¼ cup chopped fresh basil or oregano *or* 1 teaspoon dried basil or oregano leaves

2 tablespoons toasted slivered almonds*

Garlic Toasts (recipe follows)

To toast almonds, place almonds in shallow baking pan. Bake in preheated 350°F oven about 10 minutes or until lightly toasted, stirring occasionally. (Watch almonds carefully—they burn easily.)

1. Combine cottage cheese, blue cheese, garlic and lemon juice in food processor; process until smooth. Add green onions, basil and almonds; pulse until well blended but still chunky.

2. Spoon cheese spread into small serving bowl; cover. Refrigerate until ready to serve.

3. When ready to serve, prepare Garlic Toasts. Spread 1 tablespoon cheese spread onto each toast slice. Garnish, if desired.

Makes 16 servings

Garlic Toasts

32 French bread slices, ½ inch thick

Nonstick cooking spray

¼ teaspoon garlic powder

⅛ teaspoon salt

Place bread slices on nonstick baking sheet. Lightly coat both sides of bread slices with nonstick cooking spray. Combine garlic powder and salt in small bowl; sprinkle evenly onto bread slices. Broil, 6 to 8 inches from heat, 30 to 45 seconds on each side or until bread slices are lightly toasted on both sides.

Makes 32 pieces

Herbed Blue Cheese Spread with Garlic Toasts

Nutty Carrot Spread

6 ounces cream cheese, softened

2 tablespoons frozen orange juice concentrate, thawed

¼ teaspoon ground cinnamon

1 cup shredded carrot

¼ cup finely chopped pecans, toasted

¼ cup raisins

36 party pumpernickel bread slices, toasted, or melba toast rounds

1. Combine cream cheese, orange juice concentrate and cinnamon in small bowl; stir until well blended. Stir in carrot, pecans and raisins.

2. Spread about 1 tablespoon cream cheese mixture onto each bread slice.

Makes 18 servings

Tip: To toast pecans, place in shallow baking pan. Bake at 350°F 10 minutes or until lightly toasted, stirring occasionally.

Guacamole

2 large avocados, pitted and peeled

¼ cup finely chopped tomato

2 tablespoons lime juice or lemon juice

2 tablespoons grated onion with juice

½ teaspoon salt

¼ teaspoon hot pepper sauce

Black pepper to taste

Additional chopped tomato (optional)

Place avocados in medium bowl; mash coarsely with fork. Stir in tomato, lime juice, onion with juice, salt and pepper sauce; mix well. Add black pepper. Spoon into serving container. Serve immediately or cover and refrigerate up to 2 hours. Garnish with additional chopped tomato, if desired.

Makes 2 cups

Tip: To quickly ripen hard avocados, store them in a loosely closed paper bag at room temperature.

Nutty Carrot Spread

Broccoli Dip

Prep Time: 5 minutes   **Microwave Time:** 6 minutes

1 package (10 ounces) frozen chopped broccoli

1 pound (16 ounces) VELVEETA® Pasteurized Prepared Cheese Product, cut up

⅛ teaspoon garlic powder

1. Microwave broccoli in covered 2-quart microwavable bowl on HIGH 3 minutes or until thawed; drain.

2. Add Velveeta and garlic powder. Microwave 2 to 3 minutes or until Velveeta is melted, stirring after 2 minutes. Serve hot with crackers and assorted cut-up vegetables.   *Makes 2¾ cups*

Serving Suggestion: Try serving Broccoli Dip in an edible bread bowl. Cut a lengthwise slice from the top of a 1-pound round or oval bread loaf. Remove bread from center, leaving a 1-inch-thick bread shell. Pour in your hot Broccoli Dip and serve.

Vegetable-Topped Hummus

1 can (15 ounces) chick-peas, rinsed and drained

2 tablespoons tahini

2 tablespoons lemon juice

1 clove garlic

¾ teaspoon salt

1 tomato, finely chopped

2 green onions, chopped

2 tablespoons chopped fresh parsley

1. In food processor or blender combine chick-peas, tahini, lemon juice, garlic and salt; process until smooth.

2. Combine tomato, onions and parsley in small bowl.

3. Place bean mixture in medium serving bowl; spoon tomato mixture evenly over top. Serve with wedges of pita bread or assorted crackers.   *Makes 8 servings*

Broccoli Dip

Mildly Wild Chili con Queso

½ **pound lean ground beef**

½ **cup chopped onion**

2 **can (15 ounces) WOLF BRAND® Mild Chili with Beans**

¼ **cup picante sauce, medium**

1 **can (15 ounces) pinto beans, drained and rinsed**

1 **cup low fat pepper jack cheese**

1 **pound low fat, low sodium, pasteurized process cheese spread**

1 **cup chopped tomatoes**

½ **cup sliced green onions**

Reduced fat tortilla chips *or* fresh vegetables

1. In large skillet, brown ground beef with onion until no longer pink; drain.

2. Add Wolf Chili and *remaining* ingredients *except* chips or fresh vegetables; heat through over medium-low heat until cheese has melted.

3. Serve with tortilla chips or fresh vegetables.

Makes 20 (½-cup) servings

Helpful Hint

The leanest cuts of ground beef are ground round and ground sirloin at about 11 percent fat; these are also the most expensive. Ground chuck contians about 15 to 20 percent fat and is more moderately priced. Store ground beef, lightly wrapped, in the coldest part of the refrigerator for up to two days.

Roasted Garlic Hummus

2 tablespoons Roasted Garlic (recipe follows)

1 can (15 ounces) chick-peas, rinsed and drained

¼ cup fresh parsley, stems removed

2 tablespoons lemon juice

2 tablespoons water

½ teaspoon curry powder

3 drops dark sesame oil

Dash hot pepper sauce

Pita bread (optional)

Prepare Roasted Garlic. Place chick-peas, parsley, 2 tablespoons Roasted Garlic, lemon juice, water, curry powder, sesame oil and hot pepper sauce in food processor or blender; process until smooth, scraping down side of bowl once. Serve with pita bread triangles, if desired.

Makes 6 (¼-cup) servings

Roasted Garlic: Cut off top third of 1 large garlic head (not the root end) to expose cloves; discard top. Place head of garlic, trimmed end up, on 10-inch square of foil. Rub garlic generously with olive oil and sprinkle with salt. Gather foil ends together and close tightly. Roast in preheated 350°F oven 45 minutes or until cloves are golden and soft. When cool enough to handle, squeeze roasted garlic cloves from skins; discard skins.

Prize-Winning Party-Size Bean Dip

2 cans (15 ounces each) black beans, rinsed and drained

1 can (15 ounces) refried beans

1 small jar (12 ounces) chunky salsa

1 package (4 ounces) crumbled feta cheese (plain or flavored)

½ cup chopped fresh cilantro

Combine all ingredients in serving bowl; mix well. Refrigerate at least 1 hour to blend flavors. Serve with tortilla chips.

Makes about 6 cups dip

Nutty Broccoli Spread

Prep Time: 10 minutes   **Cook Time:** 10 to 15 minutes

1 box (10 ounces) BIRDS EYE® frozen Chopped Broccoli

4 ounces cream cheese

¼ cup grated Parmesan cheese

1 teaspoon dried basil

¼ cup walnuts

1 loaf frozen garlic bread

- Cook broccoli according to package directions; drain well.

- Preheat oven to 400°F. Place broccoli, cream cheese, Parmesan cheese and basil in food processor or blender; process until ingredients are mixed. (Do not overmix.) Add walnuts; process 3 to 5 seconds.

- Split garlic bread lengthwise. Spread broccoli mixture evenly over bread.

- Bake 10 to 15 minutes or until bread is toasted and broccoli mixture is heated through.

- Cut bread into bite-size pieces; serve hot.

Makes about 2 cups spread

Maple Dijon Dip

1 cup HIDDEN VALLEY® Original Ranch® Dressing

4 teaspoons pure maple syrup

1 teaspoon Dijon mustard

Hot cooked chicken nuggets (optional)

Stir together dressing, syrup and mustard in a small bowl. Chill 30 minutes. Serve with chicken nuggets, if desired.   *Makes 1 cup*

Nutty Broccoli Spread

Cowboy Caviar

Nonstick cooking spray

2 teaspoons olive oil

1 small eggplant (about ¾ pound), peeled and chopped

1 cup chopped onion

1 jalapeño pepper,* seeded and finely chopped (optional)

1 can (15 ounces) salsa-style chunky tomatoes, undrained

1 can (15 ounces) black-eyed peas, rinsed and drained

1 teaspoon ground cumin

½ cup minced fresh cilantro

Baked tortilla chips

*Jalapeño peppers can sting and irritate the skin; wear rubber gloves when handling peppers and do not touch eyes. Wash hands after handling.

1. Coat large nonstick skillet with cooking spray. Add oil; heat over medium heat until hot. Add eggplant, onion and jalapeño pepper, if desired; cook and stir 10 minutes or until vegetables are tender.

2. Stir in tomatoes with juices, black-eyed peas and cumin. Cook 5 minutes, stirring frequently. Remove from heat; stir in cilantro.

3. Serve with tortilla chips. *Makes 16 servings*

Helpful Hint

Purchase firm eggplants with smooth skin that are heavy for their size. Eggplants should be stored in a cool, dry place and used within a few days of purchase, as they are quite perishable and will develop soft spots and a bitter taste with age.

Cowboy Caviar

Santa Fe Pineapple Salsa

Prep Time: 20 minutes   **Chill Time:** 30 minutes

2 cups finely chopped DOLE®
    Fresh Pineapple

1 can (8 ounces) red, pinto
    or kidney beans, drained
    and rinsed

1 can (8¼ ounces) whole
    kernel corn, drained

1 cup chopped DOLE® Red or
    Green Bell Pepper

½ cup finely chopped DOLE®
    Red Onion

2 tablespoons chopped fresh
    cilantro

1 to 2 teaspoons seeded and
    chopped fresh jalapeño
    pepper

½ teaspoon grated lime peel

2 tablespoons lime juice

• Combine pineapple, beans, corn, bell pepper, onion, cilantro, jalapeño, lime peel and juice in medium serving bowl. Cover and chill at least 30 minutes to allow flavors to blend. Serve as a dip with tortilla chips or spoon over quesadillas or tacos. Garnish with grilled pineapple wedges, if desired. *Makes 10 servings*

Helpful Hint

To peel and cut a pineapple, use a very sharp knife and cut off both the base and the leaves. Stand the pineapple on one end and remove the skin in strips, cutting from top to bottom. Cut the peeled pineapple vertically in quarters, then cut down the length of each quarter to remove the core.

Feta Avocado Spread

4 ripe avocados, peeled and cut into chunks

1 (4-ounce) package feta cheese, crumbled

1 tablespoon olive oil

Juice of 1 lemon

2 teaspoons TABASCO® brand Green Pepper Sauce

Salt to taste

1 baguette French bread *or* 2 heads Belgian endive (optional)

Combine avocados, feta cheese, oil, lemon juice, TABASCO® Green Pepper Sauce and salt in medium bowl. Mix with fork until well blended and still slightly lumpy. Spoon into serving bowl and refrigerate until ready to serve.

Serve with sliced baguette rounds, if desired. For more elegant presentation, spoon small amount of spread on larger ends of endive leaves and arrange on platter.

Makes 3½ cups

Spinach Dip

Preparation Time: 10 minutes   **Chill Time:** 1 hour   **Total Time:** 1 hour and 10 minutes

1 (16-ounce) container BREAKSTONE'S® or KNUDSEN® Sour Cream

1 (10-ounce) package frozen chopped spinach, thawed and well drained

¼ cup chopped red pepper

¼ cup chopped green onions

1 clove garlic, crushed

½ teaspoon hot pepper sauce

WHEAT THINS® Snack Crackers

1. Blend sour cream, spinach, red pepper, green onions, garlic and pepper sauce in bowl. Cover; refrigerate at least 1 hour to blend flavors.

2. Serve as dip with snack crackers.

Makes 2 cups

Creamy Feta & Sun-Dried Tomato Spread

Prep Time: 10 minutes plus refrigerating

1 package (8 ounces) PHILADELPHIA® Cream Cheese, softened

1 package (4 ounces) ATHENOS® Traditional Crumbled Feta Cheese

2 tablespoons chopped fresh basil

2 tablespoons finely chopped sun-dried tomatoes

MIX all ingredients. Refrigerate.

SERVE as a spread on NABISCO® Crackers or fresh vegetables.

Makes 1 ½ cups

Roasted Red Pepper Dip

Preparation Time: 15 minutes **Chill Time:** 1 hour **Total Time:** 1 hour and 15 minutes

1 (8-ounce) container BREAKSTONE'S® or KNUDSEN® Sour Cream

1 (7-ounce) jar roasted red peppers, drained

4 ounces PHILADELPHIA® Cream Cheese

½ teaspoon chopped fresh or frozen chives

Fresh chives, for garnish

WHEAT THINS® Snack Crackers

1. Blend sour cream, peppers, cream cheese and chopped chives with electric mixer until well mixed.

2. Spoon into bowl; refrigerate for at least 1 hour.

3. Garnish with chives if desired. Serve as dip with snack crackers.

Makes 2 cups

Creamy Feta & Sun-Dried Tomato Spread

Party Favorites

Bacon-Wrapped Breadsticks

8 slices bacon

16 garlic-flavored breadsticks (about 8 inches long)

¾ cup grated Parmesan cheese

2 tablespoons chopped fresh parsley (optional)

Cut bacon slices in half lengthwise. Wrap half slice of bacon diagonally around each breadstick. Combine Parmesan and parsley in shallow dish; set aside.

Place 4 breadsticks on double layer of paper towels in microwave oven. Microwave on HIGH 2 to 3 minutes or until bacon is cooked through. Immediately roll breadsticks in Parmesan mixture to coat. Repeat with remaining breadsticks. *Makes 16 breadsticks*

Bacon-Wrapped Breadsticks

Southwestern Quesadillas

3 (8-inch) flour tortillas

I CAN'T BELIEVE IT'S NOT BUTTER!® Spray

¼ teaspoon chili powder, divided

⅛ teaspoon ground cumin, divided

1 cup shredded Monterey Jack or cheddar cheese (about 4 ounces)

1 can (4 ounces) chopped green chilies, drained

1 can (2¼ ounces) sliced pitted ripe olives, drained

2 tablespoons chopped cilantro (optional)

Generously spray one side of one tortilla with I Can't Believe It's Not Butter! Spray. Sprinkle with ½ of the chili powder and cumin. On baking sheet, arrange tortilla spice-side down, then top with ½ of the cheese, chilies, olives and cilantro. Top with second tortilla. Repeat layers, ending with tortilla. Spray top tortilla generously with I Can't Believe It's Not Butter! Spray, then sprinkle with remaining chili powder and cumin. Grill or broil until tortillas are golden and cheese is melted. Cut in wedges and serve, if desired, with salsa.

Makes 4 servings

Helpful Hint

Monterey Jack is a mild-flavored semi-soft cow's milk cheese, made from whole, partly skimmed or skimmed milk. It has a high moisture content and is an excellent melting cheese, making it a favorite ingredient in quesadillas, sandwiches and casseroles.

Southwestern Quesadillas

Extra Special Spinach Dip

1 envelope LIPTON® RECIPE SECRETS® Vegetable Soup Mix*

1 container (8 ounces) regular or light sour cream

1 cup regular or light mayonnaise

1 package (10 ounces) frozen chopped spinach, thawed and squeezed dry

1 can (8 ounces) water chestnuts, drained and chopped (optional)

*Also terrific with LIPTON® RECIPE SECRETS® Savory Herb with Garlic Soup Mix.

1. In medium bowl, combine all ingredients; chill at least 2 hours.

2. Serve with your favorite dippers. *Makes 3 cups dip*

Helpful Hint

Water chestnuts are the edible fruit of an aquatic plant native to Southeast Asia. They are encased in a black skin that must be peeled away; the flesh inside is crisp, white and slightly sweet. The bulk of the American supply comes canned either whole or sliced. Typically used as an ingredient in stir-fries, water chestnuts are also added to dips, salads, pilafs and entrées for their crunchiness.

Extra Special Spinach Dip

Original Buffalo Chicken Wings

Prep Time: 10 minutes   **Cook Time:** 15 minutes

**Zesty Blue Cheese Dip
(recipe follows)**

**2 ½ pounds chicken wings, split
and tips discarded**

**½ cup *Frank's®* *RedHot®*
Cayenne Pepper Sauce
(or to taste)**

**⅓ cup butter or margarine,
melted**

Celery sticks

1. Prepare Zesty Blue Cheese Dip.

2. Deep fry* wings at 400°F 12 minutes or until crisp and no longer pink; drain.

3. Combine ***Frank's RedHot*** and butter in large bowl. Add wings to sauce; toss to coat evenly. Serve with Zesty Blue Cheese Dip and celery.   *Makes 24 to 30 individual pieces*

Or, prepare wings using one of the cooking methods below. Add wings to sauce; toss well to coat completely.

To Bake: Place wings in a single layer on rack in foil-lined roasting pan. Bake at 425°F 1 hour or until crisp and no longer pink, turning halfway through baking time.

To Broil: Place wings in a single layer on rack in foil-lined roasting pan. Broil 6 inches from heat 15 to 20 minutes or until crisp and no longer pink, turning once.

To Grill: Place wings on an oiled grid. Grill, over medium heat, 30 to 40 minutes or until crisp and no longer pink, turning often.

Zesty Blue Cheese Dip

½ cup blue cheese salad dressing

¼ cup sour cream

2 teaspoons *Frank's® RedHot®* Cayenne Pepper Sauce

Combine all ingredients in medium serving bowl; mix well. Garnish with crumbled blue cheese, if desired.   *Makes ¾ cup dip*

Shanghai Red Wings: Cook chicken wings as directed on page 50. Combine ¼ cup soy sauce, 3 tablespoons honey, 3 tablespoons **Frank's RedHot**, 2 tablespoons peanut oil, 1 teaspoon grated peeled fresh ginger and 1 teaspoon minced garlic in small bowl. Mix well. Pour sauce over wings; toss well to coat evenly.

Cajun Wings: Cook chicken wings as directed on page 50. Combine ⅓ cup **Frank's RedHot**, ⅓ cup ketchup, ¼ cup (½ stick) melted butter or margarine and 2 teaspoons Cajun seasoning in small bowl. Mix well. Pour sauce over wings; toss well to coat evenly.

Santa Fe Wings: Cook chicken wings as directed on page 50. Combine ¼ cup (½ stick) melted butter or margarine, ¼ cup **Frank's RedHot**, ¼ cup chili sauce and 1 teaspoon chili powder in small bowl. Mix well. Pour sauce over wings; toss well to coat evenly.

Sweet 'n' Spicy Wings: Cook chicken wings as directed on page 50. Combine ⅓ cup **Frank's RedHot**, ¼ cup (½ stick) butter, 2 tablespoons each frozen thawed orange juice concentrate and honey, and ¼ teaspoon each ground cinnamon and ground allspice in small microwavable bowl. Microwave on HIGH 1 minute or until butter is melted. Stir until smooth. Pour sauce over wings; toss well to coat evenly.

Oven-Fried Tex-Mex Onion Rings

½ cup plain dry bread crumbs

⅓ cup yellow cornmeal

1 ½ teaspoons chili powder

⅛ to ¼ teaspoon ground red pepper

⅛ teaspoon salt

1 tablespoon plus
   1 ½ teaspoons margarine, melted

2 medium onions (about
   10 ounces), sliced ⅜ inch thick

2 egg whites

1. Preheat oven to 450°F. Spray large nonstick baking sheet with nonstick cooking spray; set aside.

2. Combine bread crumbs, cornmeal, chili powder, pepper and salt in medium shallow dish; mix well. Stir in margarine and 1 teaspoon water.

3. Separate onion slices into rings. Place egg whites in large bowl; beat lightly. Add onions; toss lightly to coat evenly. Transfer to bread crumb mixture; toss to coat evenly. Place in single layer on prepared baking sheet.

4. Bake 12 to 15 minutes or until onions are tender and coating is crisp.

Makes 6 servings

Oven-Fried Tex-Mex Onion Rings

Artichoke Frittata

1 can (14 ounces) artichoke
   hearts, drained and
   rinsed
1 tablespoon olive oil,
   divided
½ cup minced green onions
5 eggs
½ cup (2 ounces) shredded
   Swiss cheese
2 tablespoons grated
   Parmesan cheese
1 tablespoon minced fresh
   parsley
1 teaspoon salt
   Freshly ground pepper to
   taste

1. Chop artichoke hearts; set aside.

2. Heat 2 teaspoons oil in 10-inch skillet over medium heat. Add green onions; cook and stir until tender. Remove from skillet.

3. Beat eggs in medium bowl until light. Stir in artichokes, green onions, cheeses, parsley, salt and pepper.

4. Heat remaining 1 teaspoon oil in same skillet over medium heat. Pour egg mixture into skillet. Cook 4 to 5 minutes or until bottom is lightly browned. Place large plate over skillet and invert frittata onto plate. Return frittata, uncooked side down, to skillet. Cook about 4 minutes more or until center is just set. Cut into small wedges. *Makes 12 to 16 appetizer servings*

Helpful Hint

A fritatta is an Italian omelet, made with the ingredients mixed with the eggs before cooking instead of being folded inside. Fritattas are firmer than French omelets because they are cooked slowly over low heat; they may be flipped over to cook both sides or the top can be browned under a broiler.

Artichoke Frittata

Southwestern Potato Skins Olé

6 large baking potatoes, scrubbed

¾ pound ground beef

⅔ cup water

1 package (1 ounce) taco seasoning

½ cup sliced green onions

1 tomato, chopped

1 can (2 ¼ ounces) sliced black olives, drained

1 cup (4 ounces) shredded Cheddar cheese

2 cups Quick Taco Dip (recipe follows)

1. Pierce potatoes with fork. Microwave at HIGH 30 minutes, turning over after 15 minutes; let cool. Cut in half and scoop out potatoes, leaving ¼-inch shell. Reserve potato insides for another use.

2. Cook and stir ground beef in large skillet over medium-high heat until crumbly and no longer pink. Drain off drippings. Stir in water and taco seasoning; bring to a boil. Reduce heat to low; cook, uncovered, 15 minutes. Stir in green onions. Preheat broiler.

3. Spoon meat mixture into potato shells; top with tomato, olives and cheese. Place filled potato shells on baking sheet and heat under broiler until cheese is melted. Top with Quick Taco Dip.

Makes 6 servings

Quick Taco Dip: Combine 2 cups sour cream and 1 package (1 ounce) taco seasoning in medium bowl; mix well. Refrigerate until ready to serve. Makes 2 cups.

Can't Get Enough Chicken Wings

18 chicken wings (about
   3 pounds)

1 envelope LIPTON® RECIPE
   SECRETS® Savory Herb
   with Garlic Soup Mix

½ cup water

2 to 3 teaspoons hot pepper
   sauce* (optional)

2 tablespoons margarine or
   butter

*Use more or less according to taste
desired.

1. Cut tips off chicken wings (save tips for soup). Cut chicken wings in half at joint. Deep fry, bake or broil until golden brown and crunchy.

2. Meanwhile, in small saucepan, combine savory herb with garlic soup mix, water and hot pepper sauce. Cook over low heat, stirring occasionally, 2 minutes or until thickened. Remove from heat and stir in margarine.

3. In large bowl, toss cooked chicken wings with hot soup mixture until evenly coated. Serve, if desired, over greens with cut-up celery.

Makes 36 appetizers

Garlic Cheese Bread

2 tablespoons I CAN'T
   BELIEVE IT'S NOT
   BUTTER!® Spread—tub
   or stick

1 clove garlic, finely chopped

1 loaf French or Italian bread
   (about 12 inches long),
   halved lengthwise

¼ cup shredded mozzarella
   cheese (about 2 ounces)

2 tablespoons grated
   Parmesan cheese

Preheat oven to 350°F.

In small bowl, blend I Can't Believe It's Not Butter! Spread and garlic. Evenly spread bread with garlic mixture, then sprinkle with cheeses.

On baking sheet, arrange bread and bake 10 minutes or until bread is golden and cheeses are melted. Slice and serve.

Makes 2 servings

Hot Artichoke Dip

Prep: 15 minutes   **Bake:** 25 minutes

- 1 package (8 ounces) PHILADELPHIA® Cream Cheese, softened
- 1 can (14 ounces) artichoke hearts, drained, chopped
- ½ cup KRAFT® Mayo Real Mayonnaise
- ½ cup KRAFT® 100% Grated Parmesan Cheese
- 1 clove garlic, minced

MIX all ingredients with electric mixer on medium speed until well blended. Spoon into 9-inch pie plate or quiche dish.

BAKE at 350°F for 20 to 25 minutes or until very lightly browned.

SERVE with NABISCO® Crackers, vegetable dippers or baked pita bread wedges.
Makes 2½ cups

Special Extras: To make baked pita bread wedges, cut each of 3 split pita breads into 8 triangles. Place on cookie sheet. Bake at 350°F for 10 to 12 minutes or until crisp.

Stuffed Mushrooms

- 1 package (6 ounces) STOVE TOP® Chicken Flavor Stuffing Mix
- 24 large mushrooms (about 1½ pounds)
- ¼ cup (½ stick) butter or margarine
- ¼ cup each finely chopped red and green pepper
- 3 tablespoons butter or margarine, melted

Prepare stuffing mix as directed on package, omitting butter. Remove stems from mushrooms; chop stems. Melt ¼ cup butter in skillet. Add mushroom caps; cook and stir until lightly browned. Arrange in shallow baking pan. Cook and stir chopped mushroom stems and peppers in skillet until tender; stir into prepared stuffing. Spoon onto mushroom caps; drizzle with 3 tablespoons butter. Place under preheated broiler for 5 minutes to heat through.

Makes 12 appetizer servings

Hot Artichoke Dip

Onion and Chili Cheese Quesadillas

Prep Time: 20 minutes   **Cook Time:** 15 minutes

1 package (8 ounces) cream cheese, softened

¼ cup chopped fresh cilantro

1 tablespoon *Frank's® RedHot®* Cayenne Pepper Sauce

1 teaspoon chili powder

6 flour tortillas (6 inches)

1 ⅓ cups *French's® Taste Toppers™* French Fried Onions

Salsa (optional)

Combine cream cheese, cilantro, **Frank's RedHot** and chili powder in medium bowl; mix until smooth.

Place tortillas on sheet of waxed paper. Spread about 3 tablespoons cheese mixture on lower half of each tortilla. Sprinkle **Taste Toppers** evenly over cheese mixture. Fold tortillas in half, pressing firmly.

Heat nonstick skillet over medium heat; spray with nonstick cooking spray. Place 2 quesadillas in skillet. Cook, pressing down with spatula, about 2 minutes per side or until tortillas brown slightly. Repeat with remaining quesadillas.

To serve, cut each quesadilla in half. Serve with salsa, if desired.

Makes 6 servings

Sweet & Sour Cocktail Meatballs

1 pound ground turkey

¾ cup plain dry bread crumbs

½ cup GREY POUPON® Dijon Mustard, divided

½ cup chopped green onions, divided

1 egg, beaten

½ teaspoon ground ginger

½ teaspoon ground black pepper

1 (8-ounce) can pineapple chunks, undrained

⅓ cup firmly packed light brown sugar

¼ cup apple cider vinegar

¼ cup diced red bell pepper

1 teaspoon cornstarch

Combine turkey, bread crumbs, ¼ cup mustard, ¼ cup green onions, egg, ginger and black pepper in large bowl. Shape into 32 (1-inch) balls. Place in greased 13×9×2-inch baking pan. Bake at 350°F for 20 minutes.

Combine pineapple chunks with juice, sugar, vinegar, red bell pepper, cornstarch and remaining mustard and green onions in medium saucepan. Cook over medium heat until sauce thickens and begins to boil. Spoon pineapple sauce over meatballs. Bake 5 to 7 minutes more or until meatballs are done. Spoon into serving dish and serve with toothpicks.   *Makes 32 appetizers*

Helpful Hint

Vinegar is an essential part of sweet and sour dishes. Cider vinegar, made from fermented apple cider, has a fruity flavor that is very popular in the United States. Cider vinegar and other varieties should be stored in a cool, dark place. Once opened, it can be stored for about 6 months. (It can keep indefinitely unopened.)

Artichoke Crostini

Prep and Cook Time: 25 minutes

1 jar (6 ounces) marinated artichoke hearts, drained and chopped

3 green onions, chopped

5 tablespoons grated Parmesan cheese, divided

2 tablespoons mayonnaise

12 slices French bread (½ inch thick)

1. Preheat broiler. Combine artichokes, green onions, 3 tablespoons cheese and mayonnaise in small bowl; mix well.

2. Arrange bread slices on baking sheet. Broil 4 to 5 inches from heat source 2 to 3 minutes on each side or until lightly browned.

3. Remove baking sheet from broiler. Spoon about 1 tablespoon artichoke mixture on each bread slice and sprinkle with remaining 2 tablespoons cheese. Broil 1 to 2 minutes or until cheese is melted and lightly browned. *Makes 4 servings*

Tip: Garnish crostini with red bell pepper, if desired.

Lit'l Party Delights

¾ cup chili sauce

¾ cup grape jelly

4 teaspoons red wine

2 teaspoons dry mustard

1 ½ teaspoons soy sauce

½ teaspoon ground ginger

½ teaspoon ground cinnamon

½ teaspoon ground nutmeg

1 pound HILLSHIRE FARM® Lit'l Smokies

Combine chili sauce, jelly, wine, mustard, soy sauce, ginger, cinnamon and nutmeg in medium saucepan; heat and stir over medium heat until mixture is smooth. Add Lit'l Smokies; heat 5 to 6 minutes or until hot. Serve with frilled toothpicks.

Makes about 50 hors d'oeuvres

Artichoke Crostini

Tortilla Crunch Chicken Fingers

1 envelope LIPTON® RECIPE SECRETS® Savory Herb with Garlic Soup Mix

1 cup finely crushed plain tortilla chips or cornflakes (about 3 ounces)

1 ½ pounds boneless, skinless chicken breasts, cut into strips

1 egg

2 tablespoons water

2 tablespoons margarine or butter, melted

Preheat oven to 400°F.

In medium bowl, combine savory herb with garlic soup mix and tortilla chips. In large plastic bag or bowl, combine chicken and egg beaten with water until evenly coated. Remove chicken and dip in tortilla mixture until evenly coated; discard bag. On 15½×10½×1-inch jelly-roll pan sprayed with nonstick cooking spray, arrange chicken; drizzle with margarine. Bake, uncovered, 12 minutes or until chicken is done.   *Makes 12 appetizer servings*

Tip: Serve chicken with your favorite fresh or prepared salsa.

Bean Dip Olé

Prep Time: 5 minutes   **Microwave Time:** 9 minutes

1 pound (16 ounces) VELVEETA® Pasteurized Prepared Cheese Product, cut up

1 can (16 ounces) refried beans

1 can (4 ounces) chopped green chilies

1. Microwave Velveeta, beans and chilies in 2-quart microwavable bowl on HIGH 8 to 9 minutes or until Velveeta is melted, stirring every 4 minutes. Serve hot with tortilla chips.

Makes 3 cups

Tortilla Crunch Chicken Fingers

Festive Franks

1 can (8 ounces) crescent roll
   dough
5 ½ teaspoons barbecue sauce
⅓ cup finely shredded sharp
   Cheddar cheese
8 hot dogs
¼ teaspoon poppy seeds
   (optional)
   Additional barbecue sauce
   (optional)

1. Preheat oven to 350°F. Spray large baking sheet with nonstick cooking spray; set aside.

2. Unroll dough and separate into 8 triangles. Cut each triangle in half lengthwise to make 2 triangles. Lightly spread barbecue sauce over each triangle. Sprinkle with cheese.

3. Cut each hot dog in half; trim off rounded ends. Place one hot dog piece at large end of one dough triangle. Roll up jelly-roll style from wide end. Place point-side down on prepared baking sheet. Sprinkle with poppy seeds, if desired. Repeat with remaining hot dog pieces and dough.

4. Bake 13 minutes or until dough is golden brown. Cool 1 to 2 minutes on baking sheet. Serve with additional barbecue sauce for dipping, if desired.

Makes 16 servings

Festive Franks

7-Layer Mexican Dip

Prep Time: 10 minutes plus refrigerating

1 package (8 ounces)
   PHILADELPHIA® Cream
   Cheese, softened

1 tablespoon TACO BELL®
   HOME ORIGINALS® Taco
   Seasoning Mix

1 cup *each* guacamole, TACO
   BELL® HOME ORIGINALS®
   Thick 'N Chunky Salsa
   and shredded lettuce

1 cup KRAFT® Shredded Mild
   Cheddar Cheese

½ cup chopped green onions

2 tablespoons sliced pitted
   ripe olives

MIX cream cheese and seasoning mix. Spread onto bottom of 9-inch pie plate or quiche dish.

LAYER guacamole, salsa, lettuce, cheese, onions and olives over cream cheese mixture; cover. Refrigerate.

SERVE with NABISCO® Crackers or tortilla chips.

Makes 6 to 8 servings

Great Substitutes: If your family doesn't like guacamole, try substituting 1 cup TACO BELL® HOME ORIGINALS® Refried Beans.

Easy Vegetable Squares

Prep Time: 20 minutes

2 (8-ounce) cans refrigerated crescent rolls (16 rolls)

1 (8-ounce) package cream cheese, softened

1 (3-ounce) package cream cheese, softened

⅓ cup mayonnaise or salad dressing

1 teaspoon dried dill weed

1 teaspoon buttermilk salad dressing mix (¼ of 0.4-ounce package)

3 cups desired toppings (suggestions follow)

1 cup shredded Wisconsin Cheddar, Mozzarella, or Monterey Jack cheese

For crust, unroll crescent rolls and pat into 15½×10½×2-inch baking pan. Bake according to package directions. Cool.

Meanwhile, in small mixing bowl stir together cream cheese, mayonnaise, dill weed, and salad dressing mix. Spread evenly over cooled crust. Sprinkle with desired toppings and shredded Cheddar, Mozzarella or Monterey Jack cheese.   *Makes 32 appetizer servings*

Topping options: Finely chopped broccoli, cauliflower or green pepper; seeded and chopped tomato; thinly sliced green onion, black olives or celery; or shredded carrots.

Favorite recipe from **Wisconsin Milk Marketing Board**

Helpful Hint

To soften cream cheese quickly, remove from wrapper and place in a medium microwave-safe bowl. Microwave on MEDIUM (50% power) 15 to 20 seconds or until slightly softened.

Creamy Taco Dip

Prep Time: 5 minutes   **Microwave Time:** 5 minutes

1 pound (16 ounces)
   VELVEETA® Pasteurized
   Prepared Cheese
   Product, cut up
1 container (16 ounces)
   BREAKSTONE'S® or
   KNUDSEN® Sour Cream
1 package (1 ¼ ounces)
   TACO BELL® HOME
   ORIGINALS® Taco
   Seasoning Mix

1. Microwave all ingredients in 2-quart microwavable bowl on HIGH 5 minutes or until Velveeta is melted, stirring after 3 minutes. Serve hot or cold with corn chips or tortilla chips.

Makes 3½ cups

Helpful Hint

Try serving dips in an edible bread bowl. Cut a lengthwise slice from the top of a 1-pound round or oval loaf of bread. Remove the bread from the center, leaving a 1-inch-thick bread shell, and pour in the dip. The bread from the center of the loaf can be cut into chunks and served with the dip.

Creamy Taco Dip

Hot Hush Puppies

WESSON® Vegetable Oil
1 ¾ **cups cornmeal**
½ **cup all-purpose flour**
1 **teaspoon sugar**
¾ **teaspoon baking soda**
½ **teaspoon salt**
½ **teaspoon garlic salt**
½ **cup diced onion**
½ **to 1 (4-ounce) can diced jalapeño peppers**
1 **cup buttermilk**
1 **egg, beaten**

Fill a large deep-fry pot or electric skillet to half its depth with Wesson® Oil. Heat oil to 400°F. Meanwhile, in a large bowl, sift together cornmeal, flour, sugar, baking soda, salt and garlic salt; blend well. Add onion and jalapeño peppers; stir until well blended. In small bowl, combine buttermilk and egg; add to dry ingredients. Stir until batter is moist and *all* ingredients are combined. Working in small batches, carefully drop batter by heaping tablespoons into hot oil. Fry until golden brown, turning once during frying. Remove and drain on paper towels. Serve with your favorite salsa or dipping sauce.   *Makes 36 hush puppies*

Rookie Ribs

8 **pounds pork spareribs, cut into 2-rib portions**
⅔ **cup light molasses**
3 **tablespoons balsamic vinegar**
3 **tablespoons prepared mustard**
2 **tablespoons TABASCO® brand Pepper Sauce**

Place ribs in large saucepan with enough water to cover; heat to boiling over high heat. Reduce heat to low; cover and simmer 45 minutes or until ribs are tender. Drain.

Meanwhile, combine molasses, balsamic vinegar, mustard and TABASCO® Sauce in medium bowl.

Preheat broiler. Place ribs on rack in broiling pan and brush with sauce. Broil ribs about 7 to 9 inches from heat source for 15 minutes or until heated through, turning occasionally and brushing often with sauce.   *Makes 8 servings*

Hot Hush Puppies

Orange Maple Sausage Balls

1 pound BOB EVANS® Original Recipe Roll Sausage

1 small onion, finely chopped

1 small red or yellow bell pepper, finely chopped

1 egg

2 tablespoons uncooked cream of wheat cereal

½ cup maple syrup or maple-flavored syrup

3 to 5 tablespoons frozen orange juice concentrate, slightly thawed, to taste

Combine first 5 ingredients in large bowl until well blended. Shape into ¾-inch balls. Cook in large skillet over medium-high heat until browned on all sides and no longer pink in centers. Drain off drippings. Add syrup and orange juice concentrate to sausage mixture. Cook and stir over medium heat 2 to 3 minutes or until thick bubbly syrup forms. Serve hot. Refrigerate leftovers.

Makes about 24 appetizers

Serving Suggestion: Serve on party picks with sautéed mushrooms and water chestnuts. These meatballs would also make an excellent breakfast item; serve with small pancakes.

Spring Rolls

1 cup pre-shredded cabbage or coleslaw mix

½ cup finely chopped cooked ham

¼ cup finely chopped water chestnuts

¼ cup thinly sliced green onions

3 tablespoons plum sauce, divided

1 teaspoon dark sesame oil

3 (6-inch) flour tortillas

Combine cabbage, ham, water chestnuts, onions, 2 tablespoons plum sauce and sesame oil in medium bowl. Mix well. Spread remaining 1 tablespoon plum sauce evenly over tortillas. Spread about ½ cup cabbage mixture on each tortilla to within ¼ inch of edge; roll up. Wrap each tortilla tightly in plastic wrap. Refrigerate at least 1 hour or up to 24 hours before serving. Cut each tortilla diagonally into 4 pieces.

Makes 12 appetizers

Pesto-Stuffed Mushrooms

Prep and Cook Time: 20 minutes

12 medium mushroom caps

⅔ cup prepared basil pesto

¼ cup (1 ounce) grated Parmesan cheese

¼ cup chopped roasted red pepper

3 tablespoons seasoned breadcrumbs

3 tablespoons pine nuts

¼ cup (1 ounce) shredded mozzarella cheese

1. Preheat oven to 400°F. Twist off mushroom stems; reserve for another use. Place mushroom caps, stem side up, on baking sheet.

2. Combine pesto, Parmesan cheese, red pepper, breadcrumbs and pine nuts in small bowl; mix until well blended.

3. Fill mushroom caps with pesto mixture. Sprinkle each with mozzarella cheese. Bake 8 to 10 minutes or until filling is hot and cheese is melted. Serve immediately. *Makes 12 mushrooms*

Toasted Sun-Dried Tomato Bread

½ cup I CAN'T BELIEVE IT'S NOT BUTTER!® Spread— tub or stick

2 tablespoons finely chopped, drained sun-dried tomatoes packed in oil

1 shallot or small onion, finely chopped

1 clove garlic, finely chopped

1 loaf French or Italian bread (about 12 inches long), halved lengthwise

In small bowl, blend all ingredients except bread. Evenly spread bread with sun-dried tomato mixture. On baking sheet, arrange bread and broil until golden. Slice and serve.

Makes about 12 servings

Fiesta Chicken Nachos

1 tablespoon olive or vegetable oil

1 pound boneless, skinless chicken breasts

1 jar (16 ounces) RAGÚ® Cheese Creations!® Double Cheddar Sauce

1 bag (9 ounces) tortilla chips

2 green and/or red bell peppers, diced

1 small onion, chopped

1 large tomato, diced

In 12-inch skillet, heat oil over medium-high heat and cook chicken, stirring occasionally, 8 minutes or until no longer pink. Remove from skillet; cut into strips.

In same skillet, combine chicken and Ragú® Cheese Creations! Sauce; heat through.

On serving platter, arrange layer of tortilla chips, then ½ of the sauce mixture, bell peppers, onion and tomato; repeat, ending with tomato. Garnish, if desired, with chopped fresh cilantro and shredded lettuce.
Makes 4 servings

Recipe Tip: For a spicier dish, add chopped jalapeño peppers or hot pepper sauce to suit your taste.

Green, Green Guacamole

2 medium ripe avocados

2 to 3 green onions, chopped

2 tablespoons fresh lime juice

1 tablespoon TABASCO® brand Green Pepper Sauce

½ teaspoon salt

Raw vegetables *or* tortilla chips

Cut avocados in half and remove pits. Combine onions, lime juice and TABASCO® Green Pepper Sauce in medium bowl; mash gently with fork to release flavor of onions. Scoop out avocados; add to bowl and continue to mash until chunky. Stir in salt. Cover tightly with plastic wrap and refrigerate 1 hour to blend flavors. Serve with cut-up vegetables and tortilla chips.
Makes about 2 cups

Fiesta Chicken Nachos

Quick Pimiento Cheese Snacks

2 ounces cream cheese, softened

½ cup (2 ounces) shredded Cheddar cheese

1 jar (2 ounces) diced pimiento, drained

2 tablespoons finely chopped pecans

½ teaspoon hot pepper sauce

24 French bread slices, about ¼ inch thick, or party bread slices

1. Preheat broiler.

2. Combine cream cheese and Cheddar cheese in small bowl; mix well. Stir in pimiento, pecans and hot pepper sauce.

3. Place bread slices on broiler pan or nonstick baking sheet. Broil, 4 inches from heat, 1 to 2 minutes or until lightly toasted on both sides.

4. Spread cheese mixture evenly onto bread slices. Broil 1 to 2 minutes or until cheese mixture is hot and bubbly. Transfer to serving plate; garnish, if desired. *Makes 24 servings*

Cheesy Pepper & Onion Quesadillas

⅓ cup margarine

3¾ cups frozen stir-fry mix (onions, red, yellow and green peppers)

¾ teaspoon chili powder

1 package (8 ounces) cream cheese, softened

1 package (8 ounces) shredded Cheddar cheese

10 (6-inch) flour tortillas

Preheat oven to 425°F. Heat margarine in large skillet over medium heat until melted. Add stir-fry mix and chili powder. Cook and stir until tender. Drain, reserving margarine.

Beat cream cheese with electric mixer on medium speed until smooth. Add Cheddar cheese, mixing until blended. Spread 2 tablespoons cheese mixture onto each tortilla; top with pepper mixture. Fold tortillas in half; place on baking sheet. Brush with reserved margarine. Bake 10 minutes. Cut each tortilla in half. Serve warm with salsa, if desired. *Makes 20 appetizers*

Quick Pimiento Cheese Snacks

Chicken Kabobs with Thai Dipping Sauce

Prep Time: 15 minutes   **Cook Time:** 10 minutes

1 pound boneless skinless chicken breasts, cut into 1-inch cubes

1 small cucumber, seeded and cut into small chunks

1 cup cherry tomatoes

2 green onions, cut into 1-inch pieces

⅔ cup teriyaki baste & glaze sauce

⅓ cup *Frank's® RedHot®* Cayenne Pepper Sauce

⅓ cup peanut butter

3 tablespoons frozen orange juice concentrate, undiluted

2 cloves garlic, minced

Thread chicken, cucumber, tomatoes and onions alternately onto metal skewers; set aside.

To prepare Thai Dipping Sauce, combine teriyaki baste & glaze sauce, **Frank's RedHot**, peanut butter, orange juice concentrate and garlic; mix well. Reserve ⅔ cup sauce for dipping.

Brush skewers with some of remaining sauce. Place skewers on oiled grid. Grill over hot coals 10 minutes or until chicken is no longer pink in center, turning and basting often with remaining sauce. Serve skewers with reserved Thai Dipping Sauce. Garnish as desired.

Makes 6 appetizer servings

Helpful Hint

Smaller cucumbers are younger, so they have thinner skins, fewer seeds and a sweeter taste. To seed a cucumber, first cut it in half lengthwise, then scrape out the seeds with a teaspoon.

Chicken Kabobs with Thai Dipping Sauce

Devilish Eggs

12 hard-cooked eggs, peeled
    and sliced in half
    lengthwise
¼ cup nonfat yogurt
2 tablespoons mayonnaise
3 teaspoons fresh lemon
    juice
2 teaspoons Dijon mustard
1 teaspoon TABASCO® brand
    Pepper Sauce
½ cup finely chopped fresh
    herbs (such as parsley,
    basil, dill or chives)
Salt to taste
Fresh dill or chopped fresh
    chives (optional)

Remove yolks and place in bowl of food processor with yogurt, mayonnaise, lemon juice, mustard and TABASCO® Sauce; process until smooth. Stir in herbs and salt to taste.

Transfer mixture to gallon-size plastic freezer bag and work it into one corner of bag. Hold bag tightly above mixture; twist until mixture is firmly positioned. Using scissors, snip tip of bag. Holding tip over each egg half, twist bag to generously fill empty yolk cavity. Continue until all eggs are filled.

Refrigerate eggs until ready to serve. Garnish each egg with dill sprig or chopped chives, if desired. *Makes 24 halves*

Mariachi Drumsticks

1 package (1.0 ounce)
    LAWRY'S® Taco Spices
    & Seasonings
1 ¼ cups crushed tortilla chips
2 dozen chicken drumettes
Salsa
Sour cream (optional)

In large resealable plastic food storage bag, combine Taco Spices & Seasonings and chips. Dampen chicken with water and shake off excess. Place a few pieces at a time in plastic bag; shake thoroughly to coat with chips. Arrange in greased shallow baking pan. Bake in 350°F oven, uncovered, 30 to 45 minutes or until crispy.

Makes 2 dozen appetizers

Serving Suggestion: Serve with salsa and dairy sour cream for dipping.

Beefy Nachos

1 pound ground beef

¼ cup chopped onion

⅓ cup A.1.® Steak Sauce

5 cups tortilla chips

1 cup (4 ounces) shredded
   Monterey Jack cheese

   Dairy sour cream (optional)

1 cup chopped tomato
   (optional)

¼ cup diced green chilies,
   drained (optional)

¼ cup sliced pitted ripe olives
   (optional)

In large skillet, over medium-high heat, brown beef and onion; drain. Stir in steak sauce. Arrange tortilla chips on large heatproof platter. Spoon beef mixture over chips; sprinkle with cheese. Broil, 6 inches from heat source, for 3 to 5 minutes or until cheese melts. Top with sour cream, tomato, chilies and olives if desired. Serve immediately. *Makes 6 servings*

Microwave Directions: In 2-quart microwave-safe bowl, combine beef and onion; cover. Microwave at HIGH (100% power) for 5 to 6 minutes or until browned; drain. Stir in steak sauce. In 9-inch microwave-safe pie plate, layer half of each of the chips, beef mixture and cheese. Microwave at HIGH for 2 to 3 minutes or until heated through. Top with half of desired toppings. Repeat with remaining ingredients.

Black Bean Quesadillas

Nonstick cooking spray

4 (8-inch) flour tortillas

¾ cup (3 ounces) shredded Cheddar cheese

½ cup canned black beans, rinsed and drained

2 green onions, sliced

¼ cup minced fresh cilantro

½ teaspoon ground cumin

½ cup salsa

2 tablespoons plus 2 teaspoons sour cream

1. Preheat oven to 450°F. Spray large nonstick baking sheet with cooking spray. Place 2 tortillas on prepared baking sheet; sprinkle each with half the cheese.

2. Combine beans, green onions, cilantro and cumin in small bowl. Spoon mixture over cheese; top with remaining tortillas. Coat tops with cooking spray. Bake 10 to 12 minutes or until cheese is melted and tortillas are lightly browned. Cut into quarters; top each tortilla wedge with 1 tablespoon salsa and 1 teaspoon sour cream. Transfer to serving plate. *Makes 8 servings*

South-of-the-Border Meatballs

1 ¼ pounds ground beef

1 package (1.0 ounce) LAWRY'S® Taco Spices & Seasonings

¼ cup unseasoned dry bread crumbs

¼ cup finely chopped onion

¼ cup finely chopped green bell pepper

1 egg, beaten

1 ½ cups chunky salsa

In large bowl, combine all ingredients except salsa; mix well. Form into 1-inch balls. In large skillet, cook meatballs on all sides until browned; drain fat. Add salsa to skillet. Bring to a boil over medium-high heat; reduce heat to low and simmer, uncovered, 10 minutes. *Makes 6 servings*

Serving Suggestion: Garnish with cilantro if desired.

Black Bean Quesadillas

Savory Chicken Satay

Prep Time: 15 minutes   **Marinate Time:** 30 minutes   **Cook Time:** 8 minutes

1 envelope LIPTON® RECIPE SECRETS® Onion Soup Mix

¼ cup olive or vegetable oil

2 tablespoons firmly packed brown sugar

2 tablespoons SKIPPY® Peanut Butter

1 pound boneless, skinless chicken breasts, pounded and cut into thin strips

12 to 16 wooden skewers, soaked in water

1. In large plastic bag, combine soup mix, oil, brown sugar and peanut butter. Add chicken and toss to coat well. Close bag and marinate in refrigerator 30 minutes.

2. Remove chicken from marinade, discarding marinade. On large skewers, thread chicken, weaving back and forth.

3. Grill or broil chicken until chicken is no longer pink. Serve with your favorite dipping sauces. *Makes 12 to 16 appetizers*

Honey Nut Brie

¼ cup honey

¼ cup coarsely chopped pecans

1 tablespoon brandy (optional)

1 wheel (14 ounces) Brie cheese (about 5-inch diameter)

Combine honey, pecans and brandy, if desired, in small bowl. Place cheese on large round ovenproof platter or 9-inch pie plate.

Bake in preheated 500°F oven 4 to 5 minutes or until cheese softens. Drizzle honey mixture over top of cheese. Bake 2 to 3 minutes longer or until topping is thoroughly heated. *Do not melt cheese.* *Makes 16 to 20 servings*

Cheesy Potato Skins

Prep Time: 1 hour   **Cook Time:** 25 minutes

4 large baking potatoes, baked

¼ cup (½ stick) butter or margarine, melted

¼ pound (4 ounces) VELVEETA® Pasteurized Prepared Cheese Product, cut up

2 tablespoons chopped red or green bell pepper

2 slices OSCAR MAYER® Bacon, crisply cooked, crumbled

1 tablespoon sliced green onion

BREAKSTONE'S® or KNUDSEN® Sour Cream

- Heat oven to 450°F.

- Cut potatoes in half lengthwise; scoop out centers, leaving ¼-inch shells. (Reserve centers for another use.) Cut shells in half crosswise. Place on cookie sheet; brush with butter.

- Bake 20 to 25 minutes or until crisp and golden brown. Top with prepared cheese product; continue baking until prepared cheese product begins to melt. Top with remaining ingredients.

Makes 16 appetizer servings

Chicken Pesto Pizza

1 loaf (1 pound) frozen bread dough, thawed

8 ounces chicken tenders, cut into ½-inch pieces

½ red onion, cut into quarters and thinly sliced

¼ cup prepared pesto

2 large plum tomatoes, seeded and diced

1 cup (4 ounces) shredded pizza cheese blend or mozzarella cheese

Preheat oven to 375°F. Roll out bread dough on floured surface to 14×8-inch rectangle. Transfer to baking sheet sprinkled with cornmeal. Cover loosely with plastic wrap and let rise 20 to 30 minutes.

Meanwhile, spray large skillet with nonstick cooking spray; heat over medium heat. Add chicken; cook and stir 2 minutes. Add onion and pesto; cook and stir 3 to 4 minutes or until chicken is cooked through. Stir in tomatoes; remove from heat and let cool slightly.

Spread chicken mixture evenly over bread dough within 1 inch of edges. Sprinkle with cheese.

Bake on bottom rack of oven about 20 minutes or until crust is golden brown. Cut into 2-inch squares.

Makes about 20 appetizer pieces

Helpful Hint

Chicken tenders are the lean, tender strips that are found on the underside of the breast. They are skinless and boneless and have virtually no waste. Any chicken pieces, dark or white meat, can be substituted for the tenders in this recipe. Or, save time and use leftover chicken or meat from a supermarket rotisserie chicken.

Chicken Pesto Pizza

Herb Cheese Twists

Prep and Cook Time: 20 minutes

2 tablespoons butter or margarine

¼ cup grated Parmesan cheese

1 teaspoon dried parsley flakes

1 teaspoon dried basil leaves

1 can (7 ½ ounces) buttermilk biscuits

1. Preheat oven to 400°F. Microwave butter in small bowl at 50% power just until melted; cool slightly. Stir in cheese, parsley and basil. Set aside.

2. Pat each biscuit into 5×2-inch rectangle. Spread 1 teaspoon of butter mixture on each rectangle; cut each in half lengthwise. Twist each strip 3 or 4 times. Place on lightly greased baking sheet. Bake 8 to 10 minutes or until golden brown.

Makes 5 servings

Cut the time: Butter mixture can be spread on ready-to-bake bread sticks and baked according to package directions.

Bourbon Dogs

2 cups ketchup

¾ cup bourbon

½ cup dark brown sugar

1 tablespoon grated onion

1 pound HILLSHIRE FARM® Lit'l Smokies

Combine ketchup, bourbon, brown sugar and onion in medium saucepan. Stir in Lit'l Smokies; simmer in sauce over low heat or bake in 300°F oven 1 hour.* Serve hot.

Makes about 50 hors d'oeuvres

*If mixture becomes too thick, thin with additional bourbon or water.

Herb Cheese Twists

Cheesy Potato Skins with Black Beans & Salsa

6 medium potatoes (6 ounces each), baked

¾ cup GUILTLESS GOURMET® Black Bean Dip (Spicy or Mild)

¾ cup (3 ounces) grated Cheddar cheese

¾ cup GUILTLESS GOURMET® Salsa (Roasted Red Pepper or Southwestern Grill)

¾ cup low fat sour cream

Fresh cilantro sprigs (optional)

Preheat oven to 400°F. Cut baked potatoes in half lengthwise and scoop out potato pulp, leaving ¼-inch pulp attached to skin (avoid breaking skin). (Save potato pulp for another use, such as mashed potatoes.) Place potato skins on large baking sheet, skin sides down; bake 5 minutes.

Fill each potato skin with 1 tablespoon bean dip and 1 tablespoon cheese. Return to oven; bake 10 minutes. Remove from oven; let cool 5 minutes. Dollop 1 tablespoon salsa and 1 tablespoon sour cream onto each potato. Garnish with cilantro, if desired. Serve hot.

Makes 12 servings

Helpful Hint

The best variety of potatoes for baking is the Russet or Idaho potato, as they have low moisture and high starch contents. Before baking, scrub potatoes well, dry with paper towels and pierce them several times with a fork to allow steam to escape during baking.

Cheesy Potato Skins with Black Beans & Salsa

By the Handful

Sweet and Spicy Snack Mix

Prep and Cook Time: 12 minutes

6 cups popped corn

3 cups miniature pretzels

1½ cups pecan halves

⅔ cup packed brown sugar

⅓ cup butter or margarine

1 teaspoon ground cinnamon

¼ teaspoon ground red pepper

1. Combine popped corn, pretzels and pecans in large bowl.

2. Place brown sugar, butter, cinnamon and red pepper in 2-cup microwavable cup. Microwave at HIGH 1½ minutes or until bubbly.

3. Pour butter mixture over popcorn mixture; toss with rubber spatula until well mixed.

Makes about 10 cups

Sweet and Spicy Snack Mix

Peppy Snack Mix

3 plain rice cakes, broken into bite-size pieces

1½ cups bite-size frosted shredded wheat biscuit cereal

¾ cup pretzel sticks, halved

3 tablespoons reduced-fat margarine, melted

2 teaspoons low-sodium Worcestershire sauce

¾ teaspoon chili powder

⅛ to ¼ teaspoon ground red pepper

Preheat oven to 300°F. Combine rice cakes, cereal and pretzels in 13×9-inch baking pan. Combine margarine, Worcestershire, chili powder and pepper in small bowl. Drizzle over cereal mixture; toss to combine. Bake 20 minutes, stirring after 10 minutes.

Makes 6 (⅔-cup) servings

Spiced Nuts

1 egg white

2 tablespoons sugar

1 teaspoon ground cinnamon

½ teaspoon ground allspice

1¾ cups pecan halves

1. Preheat oven to 325°F. Grease baking sheet; set aside.

2. Beat egg white in small bowl with electric mixer until soft peaks form. Beat in sugar, cinnamon and allspice. Stir in pecans until coated.

3. Spread pecans on prepared baking sheet, separating pecans. Bake about 12 minutes or until crisp. Let stand until cooled.

Makes about ¼ pound

Peppy Snack Mix

Honey Popcorn Clusters

Prep Time: 20 minutes   **Bake Time:** 15 minutes

Vegetable cooking spray

6 cups air-popped popcorn

⅔ cup DOLE® Golden or
   Seedless Raisins

½ cup DOLE® Chopped Dates
   or Pitted Dates, chopped

⅓ cup almonds (optional)

⅓ cup packed brown sugar

¼ cup honey

2 tablespoons margarine

¼ teaspoon baking soda

- Line bottom and sides of 13×9-inch baking pan with large sheet of aluminum foil. Spray foil with vegetable cooking spray.

- Stir together popcorn, raisins, dates and almonds in foil-lined pan.

- Combine brown sugar, honey and margarine in small saucepan. Bring to boil over medium heat, stirring constantly; reduce heat to low. Cook 5 minutes. *Do not stir.* Remove from heat.

- Stir in baking soda. Pour evenly over popcorn mixture, stirring quickly to coat mixture evenly.

- Bake at 300°F 12 to 15 minutes or until mixture is lightly browned, stirring once halfway through baking time.

- Lift foil from pan; place on cooling rack. Cool popcorn mixture completely; break into clusters. Popcorn can be stored in airtight container up to 1 week.   *Makes 7 cups*

Easy Wonton Chips

1 tablespoon reduced-sodium
   soy sauce

2 teaspoons peanut or
   vegetable oil

½ teaspoon sugar

¼ teaspoon garlic salt

12 fresh or thawed frozen
   wonton skins

   Nonstick cooking spray

1. Preheat oven to 375°F.

2. Combine soy sauce, oil, sugar and garlic salt in small bowl; mix well.

3. Cut each wonton skin diagonally in half. Place wonton skins on 15×10-inch jelly-roll pan coated with nonstick cooking spray. Brush soy sauce mixture evenly over both sides of each wonton skin.

4. Bake 4 to 6 minutes until crisp and lightly browned, turning after 3 minutes. Transfer to cooling rack; cool completely. Store tightly covered at room temperature. *Makes 4 appetizer servings*

Party Mix

2 cups shredded wheat cereal

1 cup puffed wheat cereal

1 cup toasted oat cereal

1 cup small thin pretzels

½ cup unsalted peanuts or
   mixed nuts

3 tablespoons vegetable oil

1½ teaspoons Worcestershire
   sauce

½ to 1 teaspoon LAWRY'S®
   Garlic Powder with
   Parsley

In large bowl, combine all cereals, pretzels and nuts. In separate bowl, combine oil, Worcestershire sauce and Garlic Powder with Parsley; mix well. Pour over cereal mixture and toss to coat all dry ingredients well. Spread out evenly on a cookie sheet. Toast in 120°F oven for 40 minutes, stirring every 15 minutes. Remove and serve warm or cooled. *Makes 15 (⅓-cup) servings*

Serving Suggestion: Serve with lots of cold beverages.

Cinnamon Popcorn

Prep Time: 15 minutes   **Cook Time:** 8 to 10 minutes

10 cups air-popped popcorn (½ cup unpopped)

1½ cups (7 ounces) coarsely chopped pecans

¾ cup granulated sugar

¾ cup packed light brown sugar

½ cup light corn syrup

3 tablespoons *Frank's® RedHot®* Cayenne Pepper Sauce

2 tablespoons honey

6 tablespoons (¾ stick) unsalted butter, at room temperature, cut into thin pats

1 tablespoon ground cinnamon

1. Preheat oven to 250°F. Place popcorn and pecans in 5-quart ovenproof bowl or Dutch oven. Bake 15 minutes.

2. Combine sugars, corn syrup, *Frank's RedHot* and honey in 2-quart saucepan. Bring to a full boil over medium-high heat, stirring just until sugars dissolve. Boil about 6 to 8 minutes or until soft crack stage (290°F on candy thermometer). *Do not stir.* Remove from heat.

3. Gradually add butter and cinnamon to sugar mixture, stirring gently until well blended. Pour over popcorn, tossing to coat evenly.* Spread popcorn mixture on greased baking sheets, using two forks. Cool completely. Break into bite-size pieces. Store in airtight container up to 2 weeks.   *Makes 18 cups*

If popcorn mixture sets too quickly, return to oven to rewarm. Popcorn mixture may be shaped into 3-inch balls while warm, if desired.

Cinnamon Popcorn

Sun-Dried Tomato Pizza Snack Mix

2 cups wheat cereal squares

2 cups unsweetened puffed corn cereal

2 cups crisp rice cereal

2 cups square mini cheese crackers

1 cup roasted sunflower seeds

3 tablespoons grated Parmesan cheese

3 tablespoons butter

2 tablespoons olive oil

2 teaspoons dried Italian seasoning

1½ teaspoons garlic powder

¼ cup tomato sauce

1 teaspoon balsamic vinegar

¼ teaspoon sugar

⅛ teaspoon salt

8 to 9 sun-dried tomatoes packed in oil, diced

1. Preheat oven to 250°F. Spray 13×9-inch baking pan with nonstick cooking spray.

2. Combine cereals, cheese crackers and sunflower seeds in large bowl; set aside.

3. Combine cheese, butter, oil, Italian seasoning and garlic powder in medium bowl. Microwave at HIGH 1 to 1½ minutes until foamy and herbs release their aromas. Stir in tomato sauce, vinegar, sugar and salt. Pour over cereal mixture; stir well to coat. Place in prepared pan and spread in single layer.

4. Bake 55 to 60 minutes, stirring every 15 minutes. Stir in sun-dried tomatoes 15 minutes before finished baking. Cool in pan on wire rack about 2 hours, leaving uncovered until mixture is crisp and tomato pieces have lost their moisture. Store in airtight container or resealable plastic food storage bag.

Makes 7 cups

Sun-Dried Tomato Pizza Snack Mix

Savory Pita Chips

2 whole wheat or white pita
  bread rounds

Olive oil-flavored nonstick
  cooking spray

3 tablespoons grated
  Parmesan cheese

1 teaspoon dried basil leaves

¼ teaspoon garlic powder

1. Preheat oven to 350°F. Line baking sheet with foil; set aside.

2. Using small scissors, carefully split each pita bread round around edges; separate to form 2 rounds. Cut each round into 6 wedges.

3. Place wedges, rough side down, on prepared baking sheet; coat lightly with cooking spray. Turn wedges over; spray again.

4. Combine Parmesan cheese, basil and garlic powder in small bowl; sprinkle evenly over pita wedges.

5. Bake 12 to 14 minutes or until golden brown. Cool completely.

Makes 4 servings

Cinnamon Crisps: Substitute butter-flavored cooking spray for olive oil-flavored cooking spray, and 1 tablespoon sugar mixed with ¼ teaspoon ground cinnamon for Parmesan cheese, basil and garlic powder.

Savory Pita Chips

Deviled Mixed Nuts

3 tablespoons vegetable oil

2 cups assorted unsalted nuts, such as peanuts, almonds, Brazil nuts or walnuts

2 tablespoons sugar

1 teaspoon paprika

½ teaspoon chili powder

½ teaspoon curry powder

½ teaspoon ground cumin

½ teaspoon ground coriander

½ teaspoon black pepper

¼ teaspoon salt

Heat oil in large skillet over medium heat; cook and stir nuts in hot oil 2 to 3 minutes or until browned. Combine remaining ingredients in small bowl; sprinkle over nuts. Stir to coat evenly. Heat 1 to 2 minutes more. Drain nuts on wire rack lined with paper towels. Serve warm.

Makes 2 cups

Caramel Popcorn

1 tablespoon margarine

1 cup firmly packed light brown sugar

¼ cup water

6 cups air-popped popcorn

1. Melt margarine in medium saucepan over medium heat. Add brown sugar and water; stir until sugar is dissolved. Bring to a boil; cover and cook 3 minutes.

2. Uncover pan; continue cooking mixture to the soft-crack stage (275°F on candy thermometer). Do not overcook. Pour hot mixture over popcorn; stir with wooden spoon.

3. Spread popcorn in single layer on sheet of aluminum foil to cool. When cool, break apart.

Makes 6 (1-cup) servings

Caramel-Cinnamon Snack Mix

2 tablespoons vegetable oil

½ cup popcorn kernels

½ teaspoon salt, divided

1 ½ cups packed light brown sugar

½ cup butter or margarine

½ cup corn syrup

¼ cup red hot cinnamon candies

2 cups cinnamon-flavored shaped graham crackers

1 cup red and green candy-coated chocolate pieces

1. Grease 2 large baking pans; set aside.

2. Heat oil in large saucepan over high heat until hot. Add popcorn kernels. Cover pan. Shake pan constantly over heat until kernels no longer pop. Divide popcorn evenly between 2 large bowls. Add ¼ teaspoon salt to each bowl; toss to coat. Set aside.

3. Preheat oven to 250°F. Combine brown sugar, butter and corn syrup in heavy medium saucepan. Cook over medium heat until sugar melts, stirring constantly with wooden spoon. Bring mixture to a boil. Boil 5 minutes, stirring frequently.

4. Remove ½ of sugar mixture (about ¾ cup) from saucepan; pour over 1 portion of popcorn. Toss with lightly greased spatula until evenly coated.

5. Add red hot candies to saucepan. Stir constantly with wooden spoon until melted. Pour over remaining portion of popcorn; toss with lightly greased spatula until evenly coated.

6. Spread each portion of popcorn in even layer in separate prepared pans with lightly greased spatula.

7. Bake 1 hour, stirring every 15 minutes with wooden spoon to prevent popcorn from sticking together. Cool completely in pans. Combine popcorn, graham crackers and chocolate pieces in large bowl. Store in airtight container at room temperature up to 1 week. *Makes about 4 quarts*

Sweet Nothings Trail Mix

Prep and Cook Time: 10 minutes

5 cups rice and corn cereal
squares

1½ cups raisins

1½ cups small thin pretzel
sticks, broken into pieces

1 cup candy-coated chocolate
candy

1 cup peanuts

Combine cereal, raisins, pretzels, candy and peanuts in large resealable plastic food storage bag; shake well. Distribute evenly among decorated bags or serve in large bowl. *Makes 10 cups*

Sugared Nuts

1 cup sugar

½ cup water

2½ cups unsalted mixed nuts

1 teaspoon vanilla

Grease baking sheet; set aside.

Combine sugar and water in medium saucepan. Cook, stirring constantly, over medium heat until sugar dissolves.

Add nuts and vanilla. Cook, stirring occasionally, until water evaporates and nuts are sugary, about 12 minutes.

Spread on prepared baking sheet, separating nuts. Let stand until cooled. *Makes about 1 pound*

Sweet Nothings Trail Mix

Oriental Snack Mix

4 cups corn or rice cereal
squares

1 cup honey roasted peanuts

1 can (5 ounces) chow mein
noodles

¼ cup butter, melted

3 tablespoons teriyaki sauce

1 tablespoon dark sesame oil

1 teaspoon garlic powder

1. Preheat oven to 250°F. Grease 13×9-inch baking pan. Set aside.

2. Combine cereal, peanuts and noodles in medium bowl.

3. Whisk together butter, teriyaki sauce, oil and garlic powder in
small bowl until well blended.

4. Drizzle butter mixture evenly over cereal mixture; stir until evenly
coated.

5. Spread mixture in single layer in prepared baking pan. Bake
1 hour or until mix is lightly browned, stirring every 15 minutes.
Cool completely in pan on wire rack. Store in airtight container
at room temperature up to 2 weeks. *Makes 6 cups*

Party Mix with Cocoa

½ cup (1 stick) margarine

2 tablespoons sugar

2 tablespoons HERSHEY'S
Cocoa

3 cups bite-size crisp wheat
squares cereal

3 cups toasted oat cereal
rings

2 cups miniature pretzels

1 cup salted peanuts

2 cups raisins

1. Place margarine in 4-quart microwave-safe bowl; microwave at
HIGH (100%) 1 to 1½ minutes or until melted. Stir in sugar
and cocoa. Add cereals, pretzels and peanuts to margarine
mixture; stir until well coated. Microwave at HIGH 3 minutes,
stirring every minute. Stir in raisins. Microwave at HIGH
3 minutes, stirring every minute. Cool completely. Store in
airtight container at room temperature. *Makes 10 cups mix*

Caramelized Nuts

1 cup slivered almonds,
    pecans or walnuts

⅓ cup sugar

½ teaspoon ground cinnamon
    (optional)

¼ teaspoon grated nutmeg
    (optional)

1. To toast nuts, cook and stir in medium skillet over medium heat 9 to 12 minutes until light golden brown. Transfer to small bowl.

2. Sprinkle sugar evenly over bottom of skillet. Cook, without stirring, 2 to 4 minutes until sugar is melted. Remove from heat.

3. Quickly add nuts to skillet; sprinkle with cinnamon and nutmeg, if desired. Return to heat; stir until nuts are coated with melted sugar mixture. Transfer to plate; cool completely.

4. Place nuts on cutting board; coarsely chop. Store in airtight container up to 2 weeks. *Makes 1 cup nuts*

Note: Care should be taken when caramelizing sugar because the melted sugar can cause serious burns if spilled or splattered.

Ortega® Snack Mix

3 cups lightly salted peanuts

3 cups corn chips

3 cups spoon-size shredded
    wheat cereal

2 cups lightly salted pretzels

1 package (1.25 ounces)
    ORTEGA® Taco Seasoning
    Mix

¼ cup (½ stick) butter or
    margarine, melted

COMBINE peanuts, corn chips, shredded wheat, pretzels, seasoning mix and butter in large bowl. Toss well to coat. Store in airtight container or zipper-type plastic bag. *Makes about 20 servings*

Santa Fe Trail Mix

1½ cups pecan halves

1 cup cashews

¾ cup roasted shelled pistachio nuts

½ cup pine nuts

⅓ cup roasted sunflower seeds

3 tablespoons butter

2½ teaspoons ground cumin

¼ teaspoon garlic powder

¼ cup plus 1 tablespoon chili sauce

1 chipotle chili in adobo sauce, about 3 inches long

1 tablespoon frozen orange juice concentrate, thawed

Nonstick cooking spray

1 tablespoon dried cilantro leaves, divided

1. Preheat oven to 300°F. Line 15×10-inch baking sheet with foil; set aside.

2. Combine pecans, cashews, pistachios, pine nuts and sunflower seeds in large bowl.

3. Combine butter, cumin and garlic powder in small microwavable bowl. Microwave at HIGH 45 to 50 seconds or until butter is melted and foamy; stir to blend.

4. Place butter mixture, chili sauce, chipotle chili and orange juice concentrate in food processor or blender; process until smooth. Pour sauce over nut mixture; stir to coat evenly. Spread mixture in single layer on prepared baking sheet.

5. Bake about 1 hour, stirring every 10 minutes. Remove from oven and spray mixture evenly with cooking spray. Sprinkle 1½ teaspoons cilantro over mixture. Stir mixture and repeat with additional cooking spray and remaining cilantro. Set baking sheet on wire rack to cool. Leave uncovered at least 1 hour before storing in airtight container or resealable plastic food storage bag.

Makes 4 cups

Harvest-Time Popcorn

2 tablespoons vegetable oil

1 cup popcorn kernels

2 cans (1¾ ounces each) shoestring potatoes (3 cups)

1 cup salted mixed nuts or peanuts

¼ cup margarine, melted

1 teaspoon dill weed

1 teaspoon Worcestershire sauce

½ teaspoon lemon-pepper seasoning

¼ teaspoon garlic powder

¼ teaspoon onion salt

1. Heat oil in 4-quart saucepan over high heat until hot. Add popcorn kernels. Cover pan; shake continuously over heat until popping stops. Popcorn should measure 2 quarts. Do not add butter or salt.

2. Preheat oven to 325°F. Combine popcorn, shoestring potatoes and nuts in large roasting pan. Set aside.

3. Combine margarine, dill, Worcestershire sauce, lemon-pepper seasoning, garlic powder and onion salt in small bowl.

4. Pour evenly over popcorn mixture, stirring until evenly coated.

5. Bake 8 to 10 minutes, stirring once. Let stand at room temperature until cool. Store in airtight containers.

Makes 2½ quarts

Helpful Hint

To retain the natural moisture of unpopped popcorn, store it in an airtight container in the refrigerator or freezer. If you find a lot of unpopped kernels in your popcorn, it may be because the corn has lost its natural moisture, as dried-out kernels will not pop.

Harvest-Time Popcorn

S'More Gorp

2 cups honey graham cereal

2 cups low-fat granola cereal

2 cups crispy multi-bran cereal squares

2 tablespoons reduced-calorie margarine

1 tablespoon honey

¼ teaspoon ground cinnamon

¾ cup miniature marshmallows

½ cup dried fruit bits or raisins

¼ cup mini semisweet chocolate chips

1. Preheat oven to 275°F.

2. Combine cereals in nonstick 15×10×1-inch jelly-roll pan. Melt margarine in small saucepan; stir in honey and cinnamon. Pour margarine mixture evenly over cereal mixture; toss until cereals are well coated. Spread mixture evenly onto bottom of pan.

3. Bake 35 to 40 minutes or until crisp, stirring after 20 minutes. Cool completely.

4. Add marshmallows, fruit bits and chocolate chips; toss to mix.

Makes 16 servings

Spicy Toasted Nuts

2 tablespoons vegetable oil

1 tablespoon HEINZ® Worcestershire Sauce

1 cup pecan or walnut halves

In bowl, combine oil and Worcestershire sauce; add nuts and toss to coat. Spread nuts in shallow baking pan; drizzle with any remaining oil mixture. Bake in 325°F oven, 15 minutes, stirring occasionally. Sprinkle with salt or garlic salt, if desired.

Makes 1 cup

S'More Gorp

Easy Italian No-Bake Snack Mix

Prep Time: 10 minutes

3 tablespoons olive oil

1 tablespoon dried Italian seasoning

1 box (7 ounces) baked crispy snack crackers

4 cups small bow tie pretzels

1 can (12 ounces) cocktail peanuts

¼ cup grated Parmesan cheese

1. Combine oil and seasoning in large resealable plastic food storage bag; knead well.

2. Add crackers, pretzels and peanuts. Seal bag; shake gently to coat well with oil mixture. Add cheese. Seal bag; shake gently to combine. Snack mix can be stored in bag up to 5 days.

Makes 10 cups

Sugar 'n' Spice Nuts

4 cups assorted salted mixed nuts

2 tablespoons I CAN'T BELIEVE IT'S NOT BUTTER!® Spread, melted

3 tablespoons sugar

1 to 2 teaspoons ground red pepper

2 teaspoons dried coriander (optional)

Preheat oven to 300°F.

In large bowl, combine mixed nuts and I Can't Believe It's Not Butter! Spread; set aside.

In small bowl, blend remaining ingredients; stir into nut mixture. On ungreased baking sheet, evenly spread nut mixture.

Bake, stirring occasionally, 40 minutes or until nuts are golden.

Makes 4 cups nuts

Baked Tortilla Chips

6 (7- or 8-inch) flour tortillas *or* (6-inch) corn tortillas

Paprika, chili powder *or* cayenne pepper

1. Preheat oven to 375°F. Sprinkle 1 tortilla with water to dampen; shake off excess water. Lightly sprinkle top with paprika. Repeat with remaining tortillas. Cut each flour tortilla into 8 wedges, each corn tortilla into 6 wedges.

2. Arrange as many wedges as fit in single layer on baking sheet (edges may overlap slightly). Bake 4 minutes. Rotate sheet. Bake another 2 to 4 minutes or until chips are firm and flour tortillas are spotted with light golden color. Do not let corn tortillas brown. Remove chips to plate to cool. Repeat with remaining wedges.

Makes 6 servings

Citrus Candied Nuts

1 egg white

1½ cups whole almonds

1½ cups pecan halves

1 cup powdered sugar

2 tablespoons lemon juice

2 teaspoons grated orange peel

1 teaspoon grated lemon peel

⅛ teaspoon ground nutmeg

Preheat oven to 300°F. Generously grease 15½×10½×1-inch jelly-roll pan. Beat egg white in medium bowl with electric mixer on high speed until soft peaks form. Add almonds and pecans; stir until coated. Stir in powdered sugar, lemon juice, orange peel, lemon peel and nutmeg. Turn out onto prepared pan, spreading nuts in single layer.

Bake 30 minutes, stirring after 20 minutes. Turn off oven. Let nuts stand in oven 15 minutes. Remove nuts from pan to sheet of foil. Cool completely. Store up to 2 weeks in airtight container.

Makes about 3 cups

Honey Crunch Popcorn

Nonstick cooking spray

3 quarts (12 cups) hot air-popped popcorn

½ cup chopped pecans

½ cup packed brown sugar

½ cup honey

1. Preheat oven to 300°F. Spray large nonstick baking sheet with nonstick cooking spray.

2. Combine popcorn and pecans in large bowl; mix lightly. Set aside.

3. Combine brown sugar and honey in small saucepan. Cook over medium heat just until brown sugar is dissolved and mixture comes to a boil, stirring occasionally. Pour over popcorn mixture; toss lightly to coat evenly. Transfer to prepared baking sheet.

4. Bake 30 minutes, stirring after 15 minutes. Spray large sheet of waxed paper with nonstick cooking spray. Transfer popcorn to prepared waxed paper to cool. Store in airtight containers.

Makes 12 servings

Variation: Add 1 cup chopped, mixed dried fruit immediately after removing popcorn from oven.

Honey Crunch Popcorn

Finger Foods

Easy Nachos

4 (6-inch) flour tortillas

Nonstick cooking spray

4 ounces ground turkey

⅔ cup salsa (mild or medium)

2 tablespoons sliced green onion

½ cup (2 ounces) shredded Cheddar cheese

1. Preheat oven to 350°F. Cut each tortilla into 8 wedges; lightly spray one side of wedges with cooking spray. Place on ungreased baking sheet. Bake for 5 to 9 minutes or until lightly browned and crisp.

2. Cook ground turkey in small nonstick skillet until browned, stirring with spoon to break up meat. Drain fat. Stir in salsa. Cook until hot.

3. Sprinkle meat mixture over tortilla wedges. Sprinkle with green onion. Top with cheese. Return to oven 1 to 2 minutes or until cheese melts. *Makes 4 servings*

Serving Suggestion: Cut tortillas into shapes with cookie cutters and bake as directed.

Easy Nachos

Sunshine Chicken Drumsticks

½ cup A.1.® Steak Sauce

¼ cup ketchup

¼ cup apricot preserves

12 chicken drumsticks (about
2½ pounds)

Blend steak sauce, ketchup and preserves in small bowl with wire whisk until smooth. Brush chicken with sauce.

Grill chicken over medium heat for 20 minutes or until no longer pink, turning and brushing with remaining sauce. (Do not baste during last 5 minutes of grilling.) Serve hot. *Makes 12 appetizers*

Cheesy Sausage Tidbits

1 (12-ounce) package BOB
EVANS® Original Links

2 cups (8 ounces) shredded
sharp Cheddar cheese

1¼ cups all-purpose flour

½ cup butter or margarine,
melted

½ teaspoon paprika

⅛ teaspoon salt

Cook sausage in medium skillet until browned; drain on paper towels. Cut each link into 4 equal pieces. Preheat oven to 400°F. To prepare dough, combine cheese, flour, butter, paprika and salt; mix well. Wrap rounded teaspoon of dough around each piece of sausage, rolling dough in palms to form a ball. Place on ungreased baking sheet. Bake 15 to 20 minutes or until slightly browned. Serve hot. Refrigerate leftovers. *Makes 56 tidbits*

Note: Cheesy Sausage Tidbits may be prepared ahead, covered and refrigerated overnight or frozen up to 1 month before baking. If frozen, they may be baked unthawed.

Sunshine Chicken Drumsticks

Piña Quesadillas

Prep Time: 15 minutes   **Cook Time:** 5 minutes

1 can (8 ounces) DOLE®
  Crushed Pineapple, well
  drained

1 small tomato, chopped

2 tablespoons finely chopped
  green onion

2 tablespoons chopped
  jalapeño chiles

1 cup (4 ounces) shredded
  Monterey Jack cheese

4 (8-inch) flour tortillas

  Vegetable cooking spray

  Sour cream (optional)

- Combine drained pineapple, tomato, green onion and chiles.

- Sprinkle pineapple mixture and cheese evenly over one half of each tortilla. Fold each tortilla in half to form quesadillas, lightly pressing down.

- Place 2 quesadillas in large skillet sprayed with vegetable cooking spray. Cook over medium heat 3 to 5 minutes or until cheese melts, turning once halfway through cooking. Remove from skillet and repeat with remaining 2 quesadillas.

- Cut each quesadilla into 3 triangles. Serve with sour cream, if desired.

Makes 4 servings

Sticky Wings

24 chicken wings (about
   4 pounds)

¾ cup WISH-BONE® Italian
   Dressing*

1 cup apricot or peach
  preserves

1 tablespoon hot pepper
  sauce (optional)**

Also terrific with WISH-BONE® Robusto Italian or Just 2 Good Dressing.

**Use more or less to taste as desired.*

Cut tips off chicken wings (save tips for soup). Cut chicken wings in half at joint. For marinade, blend Italian dressing, preserves and hot pepper sauce. In large, shallow nonaluminum baking dish or plastic bag, pour ½ of the marinade over chicken wings; toss to coat. Cover, or close bag, and marinate in refrigerator, turning occasionally, 3 to 24 hours. Refrigerate remaining marinade.

Remove wings, discarding marinade. Grill or broil wings, turning once and brushing frequently with refrigerated marinade, until wings are done.

Makes 48 appetizers

Reuben Rolls

⅓ cup HELLMANN'S® or BEST FOODS® Real or Light Mayonnaise or Low Fat Mayonnaise Dressing

1 tablespoon HELLMANN'S® or BEST FOODS® Dijonnaise™ Creamy Dijon Mustard

½ teaspoon caraway seeds

1 cup (4 ounces) finely chopped cooked corned beef

1 cup (4 ounces) shredded Swiss cheese

1 cup sauerkraut, rinsed, drained and patted dry with paper towels

1 package (10 ounces) refrigerated pizza crust dough

1. Preheat oven to 425°F.

2. In medium bowl, combine mayonnaise, mustard and caraway seeds. Add corned beef, cheese and sauerkraut; toss to blend well.

3. Unroll dough onto large ungreased cookie sheet. Gently stretch to 14×12-inch rectangle. Cut dough lengthwise in half.

4. Spoon half of the filling onto each piece, spreading to within 1 inch from edges. From long side, roll each jelly-roll style; pinch to seal edges. Arrange rolls, seam side down, 3 inches apart.

5. Bake 10 minutes or until golden brown. Let stand 5 minutes. Cut into 1-inch slices. *Makes about 30 appetizers*

Pepper Cheese Cocktail Puffs

Prep and Bake Time: 30 minutes

½ **package (17¼ ounces) frozen puff pastry, thawed**

1 **tablespoon Dijon mustard**

½ **cup (2 ounces) finely shredded Cheddar cheese**

1 **teaspoon cracked black pepper**

1 **egg**

1 **tablespoon water**

1. Preheat oven to 400°F. Grease baking sheets.

2. Roll out 1 sheet puff pastry dough on well floured surface to 14×10-inch rectangle. Spread half of dough (from 10-inch side) with mustard. Sprinkle with cheese and pepper. Fold dough over filling; roll gently to seal edges.

3. Cut lengthwise into 3 strips; cut each strip diagonally into 1½-inch pieces. Place on prepared baking sheets. Beat egg and water in small bowl; brush on appetizers.

4. Bake appetizers 12 to 15 minutes or until puffed and deep golden brown. Remove from baking sheet to wire rack to cool.

Makes about 20 appetizers

Tip: Work quickly and efficiently when using puff pastry. The colder puff pastry is, the better it will puff in the hot oven. (Also, this recipe can be easily doubled.)

Pepper Cheese Cocktail Puffs

Beefy Tortilla Rolls

¼ cup GREY POUPON®
COUNTRY DIJON®
Mustard

3 ounces cream cheese,
softened

2 teaspoons prepared
horseradish

2 teaspoons chopped cilantro
or parsley

2 (10-inch) flour tortillas

1 cup torn spinach leaves

6 ounces thinly sliced deli
roast beef

1 large tomato, cut into
8 slices

Lettuce leaves

1. Blend mustard, cream cheese, horseradish and cilantro in small bowl. Spread each tortilla with half the mustard mixture. Top each with half the spinach leaves, roast beef and tomato slices. Roll up each tortilla jelly-roll fashion. Wrap each roll in plastic wrap and refrigerate at least 1 hour.*

2. Cut each roll into 10 slices; arrange on lettuce-lined platter. Serve immediately. *Makes 20 appetizers*

Tortilla rolls may be frozen. To serve, thaw at room temperature for 1 hour before slicing.

Bandito Buffalo Wings

1 package (1.25 ounces)
ORTEGA® Taco Seasoning
Mix

12 chicken wings (about
1 pound *total*)

ORTEGA® SALSA PRIMA™
THICK & CHUNKY

PREHEAT oven to 375° F. Lightly grease 13×9-inch baking pan.

PLACE seasoning mix in heavy-duty plastic or paper bag. Add 3 chicken wings; shake well to coat. Repeat until all wings have been coated. Place wings in prepared pan.

BAKE for 35 to 40 minutes or until no longer pink near bone. Serve with salsa for dipping. *Makes 6 appetizer servings*

Beefy Tortilla Rolls

Herbed Potato Chips

Olive oil-flavored nonstick cooking spray

2 medium-sized red potatoes (about ½ pound), unpeeled

1 tablespoon olive oil

2 tablespoons minced fresh dill, thyme or rosemary *or* 2 teaspoons dried dill weed, thyme or rosemary

¼ teaspoon garlic salt

⅛ teaspoon black pepper

1¼ cups sour cream

1. Preheat oven to 450°F. Spray large nonstick baking sheets with nonstick cooking spray; set aside.

2. Cut potatoes crosswise into very thin slices, about 1/16 inch thick. Pat dry with paper towels. Arrange potato slices in single layer on prepared baking sheets; coat potatoes with nonstick cooking spray.

3. Bake 10 minutes; turn slices over. Brush with oil. Combine dill, garlic salt and pepper in small bowl; sprinkle evenly onto potato slices. Continue baking 5 to 10 minutes or until potatoes are golden brown. Cool on baking sheets.

4. Serve with sour cream.   *Makes about 60 chips*

Salmon Appetizers

1 package frozen puff pastry sheets, thawed

4 ounces smoked salmon, flaked

8 ounces cream cheese, softened

2 tablespoons snipped chives

1½ teaspoons lemon juice

Preheat oven to 375°F. Cut 2-inch rounds of dough from pastry sheet; place in greased muffin cups. (Freeze remaining pastry sheet for later use.) Top dough rounds with salmon. Mix cream cheese, chives and lemon juice until creamy. Top salmon with about 1 tablespoon cream cheese mixture or pipe cream cheese over salmon, if desired. Bake 15 to 18 minutes. Serve warm.

Makes 12 appetizers

Favorite recipe from **Wisconsin Milk Marketing Board**

Herbed Potato Chips

Bruschetta Dijon

¼ cup olive oil, divided

1 clove garlic, minced

18 (¼-inch-thick) slices French bread

1½ cups chopped eggplant

½ cup chopped onion

½ cup diced red, yellow or green bell pepper

1 cup chopped tomato

¼ cup GREY POUPON® COUNTRY DIJON® Mustard

¼ cup chopped pitted ripe olives

1 teaspoon dried oregano leaves

2 tablespoons grated Parmesan cheese

Chopped parsley, for garnish

1. Blend 2 tablespoons oil and garlic. Arrange bread slices on baking sheets; brush tops with oil mixture. Set aside.

2. Sauté eggplant, onion and bell pepper in remaining oil in large skillet over medium heat until tender. Stir in tomato; cook for 2 minutes. Add mustard, olives and oregano; heat through.

3. Broil bread slices for 1 minute or until golden. Top each toasted bread slice with about 1 tablespoon vegetable mixture. Sprinkle with Parmesan cheese; garnish with parsley. Serve warm.

Makes 18 appetizers

Helpful Hint

When working with bell peppers, be sure to remove the membranes inside; these can have a bitter taste. The easiest way to chop bell peppers is to slice them in half vertically, then place the halves skin side down on a cutting board and dice or slice as the recipe directs.

South-of-the-Border Sausage Balls

1 pound BOB EVANS®
   Original Recipe Roll
   Sausage

½ cup dry bread crumbs

¼ cup finely chopped green
   bell pepper

¼ cup finely chopped onion

1 egg, beaten

3 tablespoons chopped fresh
   cilantro

1 tablespoon ground cumin

1½ cups chunky salsa

Combine all ingredients except salsa in large bowl until well blended. Shape into 1-inch balls. Cook in large skillet over medium heat until browned on all sides, turning occasionally. Drain off any drippings. Add salsa; bring to a boil over high heat. Reduce heat to low; simmer 10 minutes. Serve hot. Refrigerate leftovers.

Makes 6 servings

Pretzels with a Chicken Twist

Preparation Time: 15 minutes

2 packages BUTTERBALL®
   Chicken Breast Tenders,
   halved lengthwise

½ cup prepared honey
   mustard

2 cups crushed pretzels

Preheat oven to 400°F. Pour honey mustard into shallow bowl. Add chicken tenders and turn to coat. Discard any remaining honey mustard. Roll coated chicken in crushed pretzels. Place on baking sheet sprayed with nonstick cooking spray. Bake 5 to 8 minutes or until chicken is no longer pink in center. Serve with extra honey mustard for dipping.

Makes 32 appetizers

Spicy Tuna Empanadas

1 (3-ounces) pouch of
   STARKIST® Solid White
   or Chunk Light Tuna,
   drained and flaked

1 can (4 ounces) diced green
   chilies, drained

1 can (2¼ ounces) sliced ripe
   olives, drained

½ cup shredded sharp
   Cheddar cheese

1 chopped hard-cooked egg

Salt and pepper to taste

¼ teaspoon hot pepper sauce

¼ cup medium thick and
   chunky salsa

2 packages (15 ounces each)
   refrigerated pie crusts

Additional salsa

In medium bowl, place tuna, chilies, olives, cheese, egg, salt, pepper and hot pepper sauce; toss lightly with fork. Add ¼ cup salsa and toss again; set aside. Following directions on package, unfold crusts (roll out slightly with rolling pin if you prefer thinner crust); cut 4 circles, 4 inches each, out of each crust. Place 8 circles on foil-covered baking sheets; wet edge of each circle with water. Top each circle with ¼ cup lightly packed tuna mixture. Top with remaining circles, stretching pastry slightly to fit; press edges together and crimp with fork. Cut slits in top crust to vent. Bake in 425°F oven 15 to 18 minutes or until golden brown. Cool slightly. Serve with additional salsa. *Makes 8 servings*

Spicy Tuna Empanadas

Smoked Salmon Appetizers

¼ cup cream cheese, softened

1 tablespoon chopped fresh dill *or* 1 teaspoon dried dill weed

⅛ teaspoon ground red pepper

4 ounces thinly sliced smoked salmon or lox

24 melba toast rounds or other crackers

1. Combine cream cheese, dill and pepper in small bowl; stir to blend. Spread evenly over each slice of salmon. Roll up salmon slices jelly-roll fashion. Place on plate; cover with plastic wrap. Chill at least 1 hour or up to 4 hours before serving.

2. Using a sharp knife, cut salmon rolls crosswise into ¾-inch pieces. Place pieces, cut side down, on serving plate. Garnish each salmon roll with dill sprig, if desired. Serve cold or at room temperature with melba rounds.

Makes about 2 dozen appetizers

Reuben Bites

24 party rye bread slices

½ cup prepared Thousand Island dressing

6 ounces turkey pastrami, very thinly sliced

1 cup (4 ounces) shredded Swiss cheese

1 cup alfalfa sprouts

1. Preheat oven to 400°F.

2. Arrange bread slices on nonstick baking sheet. Bake 5 minutes or until lightly toasted.

3. Spread 1 teaspoon dressing onto each bread slice; top with pastrami, folding slices to fit bread slices. Sprinkle evenly with cheese.

4. Bake 5 minutes or until hot. Top evenly with sprouts. Transfer to serving plate; garnish, if desired. *Makes 12 servings*

Smoked Salmon Appetizers

Cheesy Artichoke Squares

Prep Time: 15 minutes plus thawing   **Cook Time:** 20 minutes

1 frozen ready-to-bake puff
   pastry sheet

3 eggs

1 (6½-ounce) jar marinated
   artichoke hearts,
   undrained

1 garlic clove, minced

1 cup VELVEETA® Mild
   Cheddar Shredded
   Pasteurized Process
   Cheese Food

2 tablespoons dry bread
   crumbs

1 tablespoon chopped
   parsley

½ teaspoon dried oregano
   leaves, crushed

¼ teaspoon hot pepper sauce

- Preheat oven to 375°F.

- Thaw pastry sheet according to package directions.

- Roll pastry into 12-inch square on lightly floured surface. With sharp knife, cut 11-inch square in center of sheet, leaving 1-inch border all the way around.

- Remove center square; place on ungreased cookie sheet. Beat one egg; lightly brush over pastry square.

- Cross two opposite corners of 1-inch border over each other and pull through to form 10-inch square. Place on outside edges of center square to form rim. Brush border with remaining beaten egg. Bake 10 minutes.

- Drain marinade from artichoke hearts into small skillet. Chop artichokes; set aside. Sauté garlic in marinade.

- Mix together remaining two eggs, beaten, artichokes, garlic mixture, process cheese food, bread crumbs, parsley, oregano and hot pepper sauce. Spoon into partially baked pastry shell. Continue baking 20 minutes or until puffed and golden brown. Cut into squares. *Makes about 1½ dozen*

Sausage Filled Wontons

1 pound BOB EVANS®
  Original Recipe Roll
  Sausage

¼ cup chopped onion

½ cup (2 ounces) shredded
  American cheese

3 ounces cream cheese

½ teaspoon dried marjoram
  leaves

¼ teaspoon dried tarragon
  leaves

30 wonton wrappers

  Vegetable oil

  Dipping sauce, such as
  plum sauce or sweet and
  sour sauce (optional)

To prepare filling, crumble sausage into large skillet. Add onion. Cook over medium heat until sausage is browned, stirring occasionally. Remove from heat; drain off any drippings. Stir in next 4 ingredients. Mix until cheeses melt. Lightly dampen 1 wonton wrapper by dipping your finger in water and wiping all the edges, making ¼-inch border around square. (To keep wrappers from drying, cover remaining wrappers with damp kitchen towel while working.) Place rounded teaspoonful sausage mixture in the middle of wrapper. Fold wrapper over filling to form triangle, sealing edges and removing any air bubbles. Repeat with remaining wrappers and filling.

Heat 4 inches oil in deep fryer or heavy large saucepan to 350°F; fry wontons, a few at a time, until golden brown. Remove with slotted spoon; drain on paper towels. Reheat oil between batches. Serve hot with dipping sauce, if desired. Refrigerate leftovers.

Makes 30 appetizers

Helpful Hint

It's helpful to have a deep-fat thermometer for deep frying to ensure that the oil is at the correct temperature. If the oil is not hot enough, the food will absorb oil and be greasy; if the oil is too hot, the food will burn. Frying food in small batches also helps control the temperature of the oil (by preventing the temperature from dropping too much).

Ham and Gouda Quesadilla Snacks

1½ cups shredded smoked
    Gouda cheese (6 ounces)

1 cup chopped ham
    (4 ounces)

½ cup pitted ripe olives,
    chopped

¼ cup minced red onion

½ cup GREY POUPON®
    COUNTRY DIJON®
    Mustard

8 (6- or 7-inch) flour tortillas

Sour cream, chopped
    peppers, sliced pitted
    ripe olives and cilantro,
    for garnish

Mix cheese, ham, olives and onion in small bowl. Spread 1 tablespoon mustard on each tortilla; spread about ⅓ cup cheese mixture over half of each tortilla. Fold tortilla in half to cover filling.

Heat filled tortillas in large nonstick skillet over medium heat for 4 minutes or until cheese melts, turning once. Cut each quesadilla into 3 wedges. Place on serving platter; garnish with sour cream, peppers, olives and cilantro. *Makes 24 appetizers*

Cherry Tomato Appetizers

1 pint cherry tomatoes
    Ice water

½ cup sliced green onions

¼ cup LAWRY'S® Lemon
    Pepper Marinade with
    Lemon Juice

In large pan of rapidly boiling water, carefully immerse tomatoes 15 seconds. Remove with slotted spoon and immediately submerge in ice water. Peel off and discard skins and stems. In large resealable plastic food storage bag, place tomatoes. Add green onions and Lemon Pepper Marinade; seal bag. Marinate in refrigerator at least 30 minutes. *Makes 4 servings*

Serving Suggestion: Serve as an appetizer with wooden picks.

Ham and Gouda Quesadilla Snacks

Roasted Garlic & Spinach Spirals

1 whole head fresh garlic

3 cups fresh spinach leaves

1 can (15 ounces) white beans, rinsed and drained

1 teaspoon dried oregano leaves

¼ teaspoon black pepper

⅛ teaspoon ground red pepper

7 (7-inch) flour tortillas

1. Preheat oven to 400°F. Trim top of garlic just enough to cut tips off center cloves; discard. Moisten head of garlic with water; wrap in foil. Bake 45 minutes or until garlic is soft and has a mellow garlicky aroma; cool. Remove garlic from skin by squeezing between fingers and thumb; place in food processor.

2. Rinse spinach leaves; pat dry with paper towels. Remove stems; discard. Finely shred leaves by stacking and cutting several leaves at a time. Place in medium bowl.

3. Add beans, oregano, black pepper and red pepper to food processor; process until smooth. Add to spinach; mix well. Spread mixture evenly onto tortillas; roll up. Trim ½ inch off ends of rolls; discard. Cut rolls into 1-inch pieces. Transfer to serving plates; garnish, if desired. *Makes 10 servings*

Tip: For best results, cover tortilla rolls and refrigerate 1 to 2 hours before slicing.

Cool Wings with Hot Sauce

Prep Time: 10 minutes   **Cook Time:** 45 minutes

18 chicken wings (about
  3 pounds)
1 envelope LIPTON® RECIPE
  SECRETS® Ranch Soup
  Mix
½ cup water
2 tablespoons margarine or
  butter
  Red or green cayenne
  pepper sauce

1. Cut tips off chicken wings (save tips for soup). Cut chicken wings in half at joints. Deep fry, bake or broil until golden brown and crunchy.

2. Meanwhile, in small saucepan, combine soup mix and water. Cook over low heat, stirring occasionally, 2 minutes or until thickened. Remove from heat and stir in margarine until melted.

3. In large bowl, toss cooked chicken wings with hot soup mixture until evenly coated. Serve with cayenne pepper sauce and, if desired, cut-up celery.

Makes 36 appetizers

Empandillas

½ pound ground beef
1 cup chopped black olives
¾ cup chopped fresh
  mushrooms
¼ cup water
1 package (1.0 ounce)
  LAWRY'S® Taco Spices
  & Seasonings
2 cans (8 ounces each)
  refrigerated crescent rolls
1 egg white, beaten

In medium bowl, combine ground beef, olives, mushrooms, water and Taco Spices & Seasonings; mix well. Roll out dough into 12-inch squares. Cut each sheet into 9 squares. Place approximately 2 teaspoons meat mixture in center of each square; moisten edges with water. Fold one corner over to form triangle and pinch edges together to seal. Brush with egg white. Place on ungreased baking sheet. Bake in 375°F oven 15 to 20 minutes or until golden brown.

Makes 18 appetizers

Serving Suggestion: Serve with guacamole and sour cream.

Hint: Stir 3 tablespoons grated cheese into filling for extra flavor.

Herbed Stuffed Tomatoes

15 cherry tomatoes

½ cup 1% low-fat cottage cheese

1 tablespoon thinly sliced green onion

1 teaspoon chopped fresh chervil *or* ¼ teaspoon dried chervil leaves, crushed

½ teaspoon snipped fresh dill *or* ⅛ teaspoon dried dill weed

⅛ teaspoon lemon pepper

Cut thin slice off bottom of each tomato. Scoop out pulp with small spoon; discard pulp. Invert tomatoes on paper towels to drain.

Combine cottage cheese, green onion, chervil, dill and lemon pepper in small bowl. Spoon into tomatoes. Serve at once or cover and refrigerate up to 8 hours.

Makes 5 servings

Chargin' Chicken Drumsticks

½ cup (1 stick) butter *or* margarine

2 tablespoons TABASCO® brand Pepper Sauce

1 tablespoon ketchup

1 teaspoon salt

16 chicken drumsticks (about 4 pounds)

1 cup bottled blue cheese dressing

Preheat broiler. Melt butter in small saucepan over low heat; stir in TABASCO® Sauce, ketchup and salt.

Place chicken drumsticks on rack in broiling pan; brush with TABASCO® Sauce mixture. Broil chicken drumsticks 7 to 9 inches from heat source for 10 minutes. Turn and brush with remaining TABASCO® Sauce mixture. Broil 10 to 15 minutes longer or until drumsticks are browned and tender. Serve with blue cheese dressing.

Makes 8 servings

Herbed Stuffed Tomatoes

Savory Sausage Mushroom Turnovers

1 (12-ounce) package frozen bulk pork sausage, thawed

1 cup chopped mushrooms

⅓ cup chopped onion

½ cup shredded Swiss cheese (2 ounces)

⅓ cup GREY POUPON® COUNTRY DIJON® Mustard

2 tablespoons diced red bell pepper

½ teaspoon dried thyme leaves

2 (8-ounce) packages refrigerated crescent dinner roll dough

1 egg, beaten

Sesame or poppy seed

1. Cook sausage, mushrooms and onion in large skillet over medium heat until sausage is cooked, stirring occasionally to break up sausage. Remove from heat; drain if necessary. Stir in cheese, mustard, bell pepper and thyme.

2. Separate each package of dough into 4 rectangles; press perforations together to seal. On floured surface, roll each rectangle into 6-inch square. Cut each square into quarters, making 32 squares total. Place 1 scant tablespoon sausage mixture on each square; fold dough over filling on the diagonal to form triangle. Press edges with fork to seal. Place on greased baking sheets.

3. Brush triangles with beaten egg and sprinkle with sesame or poppy seed. Bake at 375°F for 10 to 12 minutes or until golden brown. Serve warm.

Makes 32 appetizers

Helpful Hint

Turnovers may be prepared and refrigerated up to 1 day in advance or frozen up to 1 month. When preparing the turnovers ahead of time, don't brush them with beaten egg until just before baking.

Savory Sausage Mushroom Turnovers

Cheddar Tomato Bacon Toasts

Prep Time: 10 minutes   **Cook Time:** 10 minutes

1 jar (16 ounces) RAGÚ®
   Cheese Creations!®
   Double Cheddar Sauce

1 medium tomato, chopped

5 slices bacon, crisp-cooked
   and crumbled (about
   ⅓ cup)

2 loaves Italian bread (each
   about 16 inches long),
   each cut into 16 slices

1. Preheat oven to 350°F. In medium bowl, combine Ragú® Cheese Creations! Sauce, tomato and bacon.

2. On baking sheet, arrange bread slices. Evenly top with sauce mixture.

3. Bake 10 minutes or until sauce mixture is bubbling. Serve immediately.

Makes 16 servings

Hidden Valley® Cheese Fingers

2 small loaves (8 ounces
   each) French bread,
   cut in half lengthwise

1 package (8 ounces) cream
   cheese, softened

1 packet (1 ounce) HIDDEN
   VALLEY® Original Ranch®
   Salad Dressing & Recipe
   Mix

4 cups assorted toppings,
   such as chopped onions,
   bell peppers and
   shredded cheese

Slice bread crosswise into 1-inch fingers, leaving fingers attached to crust. Mix together cream cheese and salad dressing & recipe mix. Spread on cut sides of bread. Sprinkle on desired toppings. Broil about 3 minutes or until brown and bubbly.

Makes about 48 fingers

Cheddar Tomato Bacon Toasts

Chicken Saté

Prep Time: 25 minutes, plus marinating   **Broil Time:** 6 minutes

Chicken Kabobs (recipe follows)

1 teaspoon MAZOLA® Oil

1 teaspoon dark Oriental sesame oil

¼ cup finely chopped onion

1 clove garlic, minced

½ teaspoon grated fresh ginger

¼ teaspoon crushed red pepper (optional)

½ cup SKIPPY® Creamy Peanut Butter

¼ cup KARO® Light or Dark Corn Syrup

1 tablespoon soy sauce

1 tablespoon cider vinegar

⅔ cup milk

1. Begin preparing Chicken Kabobs.

2. Meanwhile, in small saucepan heat oils over medium heat; add onion, garlic, ginger and crushed red pepper. Stirring constantly, cook 3 to 4 minutes or until onion is translucent.

3. Stir in peanut butter, corn syrup, soy sauce and vinegar until smooth. Gradually stir in milk. Stirring constantly, bring to boil. Remove from heat. Cool slightly.

4. Serve as dipping sauce for Chicken Kabobs.

Makes 1⅓ cups sauce for about 3 dozen appetizers

Chicken Kabobs: Soak about 36 wooden skewers in water at least 20 minutes. In medium bowl combine 2 tablespoons MAZOLA® Oil and 2 tablespoons light teriyaki sauce. Cut 1 pound boneless skinless chicken breasts into 1-inch pieces; stir into teriyaki mixture. Cover and chill 30 minutes, several hours or overnight. Thread chicken onto skewers. Place on foil-lined baking sheet. Broil about 6 inches from heat, 6 to 8 minutes or until lightly browned.

Mini Sausage Quiches

½ cup butter or margarine, softened

3 ounces cream cheese, softened

1 cup all-purpose flour

½ pound BOB EVANS® Italian Roll Sausage

1 cup (4 ounces) shredded Swiss cheese

1 tablespoon snipped fresh chives

2 eggs

1 cup half-and-half

¼ teaspoon salt

Dash cayenne pepper

Beat butter and cream cheese in medium bowl until creamy. Blend in flour; refrigerate 1 hour. Roll into 24 (1-inch) balls; press each into ungreased mini-muffin cup to form pastry shell. Preheat oven to 375°F. To prepare filling, crumble sausage into small skillet. Cook over medium heat until browned, stirring occasionally. Drain off any drippings. Sprinkle evenly into pastry shells in muffin cups; sprinkle with Swiss cheese and chives. Whisk eggs, half-and-half, salt and cayenne until blended; pour into pastry shells. Bake 20 to 30 minutes or until set. Remove from pans. Serve hot. Refrigerate leftovers.

Makes 24 appetizers

Tip: Pour mixture into 12 standard 2½-inch muffin cups to make larger individual quiches. Serve for breakfast.

Brie Amandine

Preparation Time: 20 minutes   **Chill Time:** 1 hour   **Total Time:** 1 hour and 15 minutes

24 TRISCUIT® Crackers

4 ounces Brie, cut into 24 small wedges

¼ cup apricot preserves

PLANTERS® Sliced Almonds

1. Top each cracker with 1 piece of cheese, ½ teaspoon preserves and sliced almonds. Place on baking sheet.

2. Bake at 350°F for 2 to 3 minutes or until cheese melts.

Makes 24 servings

Festive Taco Cups

1 tablespoon vegetable oil

½ cup chopped onion

½ pound ground turkey or ground beef

1 clove garlic, minced

½ teaspoon dried oregano leaves

½ teaspoon chili powder or taco seasoning

¼ teaspoon salt

1¼ cups shredded taco-flavored cheese or Mexican cheese blend, divided

1 can (11½ ounces) refrigerated corn breadstick dough

Chopped fresh tomato and sliced green onion for garnish (optional)

Heat oil in large skillet over medium heat. Add onion and cook until tender. Add turkey; cook until turkey is no longer pink, stirring occasionally. Stir in garlic, oregano, chili powder and salt. Remove from heat and stir in ½ cup cheese; set aside.

Preheat oven to 375°F. Lightly grease 24 miniature (1¾-inch) muffin pan cups. Remove dough from container but do not unroll dough. Separate dough into 8 pieces at perforations. Divide each piece into 3 pieces; roll or pat each piece into 3-inch circle. Press circles into prepared muffin pan cups.

Fill each cup with 1½ to 2 teaspoons turkey mixture. Bake 10 minutes. Sprinkle tops of taco cups with remaining cheese; bake 2 to 3 minutes more until cheese is melted. Garnish with tomato and green onion, if desired. *Makes 24 taco cups*

Festive Taco Cups

Wisconsin Wings

Preparation Time: 25 minutes   **Cook Time:** 35 minutes   **Total Time:** 1 hour

18 RITZ® Crackers, finely crushed (about ¾ cup crumbs)

⅓ cup KRAFT® Grated Parmesan Cheese

1 teaspoon dried oregano leaves

½ teaspoon garlic powder

½ teaspoon paprika

⅛ teaspoon coarse ground black pepper

2 pounds chicken wings, split and tips removed

⅓ cup GREY POUPON® Dijon Mustard

1. Mix cracker crumbs, Parmesan cheese, oregano, garlic powder, paprika and pepper in shallow dish; set aside.

2. Coat chicken wing pieces with mustard; roll in crumb mixture to coat. Place on greased baking sheet.

3. Bake at 350°F for 35 to 40 minutes or until golden brown, turning pieces over halfway through baking time. Serve warm.

Makes 12 servings

Tip: Crush crackers quickly and easily by placing them in a sealed plastic food storage bag, then running a rolling pin over the bag several times to pulverize them.

Helpful Hint

If you don't have a pepper grinder or a mortar and pestle, you can still crush peppercorns to get a coarse grind. Try using a rolling pin or the side of an unopened can to crush peppercorns on a work surface, or use a heavy skillet to crush the peppercorns inside another skillet. (Do not use nonstick skillets for this.)

Wisconsin Wings

California Quesadillas

Prep Time: 20 minutes   **Cook Time:** 5 minutes

- 1 small ripe avocado
- 2 packages (3 ounces each) cream cheese, softened
- 3 tablespoons *Frank's® RedHot®* Cayenne Pepper Sauce
- ¼ cup minced fresh cilantro leaves
- 16 (6-inch) flour tortillas (2 packages)
- 1 cup (4 ounces) shredded Cheddar or Monterey Jack cheese
- ½ cup finely chopped green onions
- Sour cream (optional)

Halve avocado and remove pit. Scoop out flesh into food processor or bowl of electric mixer. Add cream cheese and *Frank's RedHot.* Cover and process, or beat, until smooth. Add cilantro; process, or beat, until well blended. Spread rounded tablespoon avocado mixture onto each tortilla. Sprinkle half the tortillas with cheese and onions, dividing evenly. Top with remaining tortillas; press gently.

Place tortillas on oiled grid. Grill over medium coals 5 minutes or until cheese melts and tortillas are lightly browned, turning once. Cut into triangles. Serve with sour cream, if desired. Garnish as desired.   *Makes 8 appetizer servings*

Note: You may serve avocado mixture as a dip with tortilla chips.

Ortega® Hot Poppers

1 can (4 ounces) ORTEGA® Whole Jalapeños, drained

1 cup (4 ounces) shredded mild Cheddar cheese

1 package (3 ounces) cream cheese, softened

¼ cup chopped fresh cilantro

½ cup all-purpose flour

2 eggs, lightly beaten

2 cups cornflakes cereal, crushed

Vegetable oil

ORTEGA® SALSA PRIMA™ Thick & Chunky

Sour cream (optional)

CUT jalapeños lengthwise into halves; remove seeds.

BLEND Cheddar cheese, cream cheese and cilantro in small bowl. Place 1 to 1½ teaspoons cheese mixture into each jalapeño half; chill for 15 minutes or until cheese is firm.

DIP each jalapeño in flour; shake off excess. Dip in eggs; coat with cornflake crumbs.

ADD vegetable oil to 1-inch depth in medium skillet; heat over high heat for 1 minute. Fry jalapeños, turning frequently with tongs, until golden brown on all sides. Remove from skillet; drain on paper towels. Serve with salsa and sour cream. *Makes 8 servings*

Fiery Chicken Bites

½ cup ketchup

1 tablespoon vegetable oil

2 to 2½ teaspoons hot pepper sauce

1½ teaspoons LAWRY'S® Lemon Pepper

1½ teaspoons LAWRY'S® Seasoned Salt

12 chicken drummettes, wings or thighs

In small saucepan, combine all ingredients except chicken. Bring just to a boil over medium-high heat; set aside. Broil chicken 5 inches from heat until no longer pink, about 8 to 10 minutes, turning once during cooking. Brush on sauce mixture; broil additional 2 minutes. *Makes 8 servings*

Serving Suggestion: Serve on bed of lettuce and garnish with lemon peel.

Mushroom Parmesan Crostini

1 tablespoon olive or vegetable oil

1 clove garlic, finely chopped

1 cup chopped mushrooms

1 loaf Italian or French bread (about 12 inches long), cut into 12 slices and toasted

¾ cup RAGÚ® Pizza Quick® Sauce

¼ cup grated Parmesan cheese

1 tablespoon finely chopped fresh basil leaves or 1 teaspoon dried basil leaves

Preheat oven to 375°F. In 8-inch nonstick skillet, heat oil over medium heat and cook garlic 30 seconds. Add mushrooms and cook, stirring occasionally, 2 minutes or until liquid evaporates.

On baking sheet, arrange bread slices. Evenly spread Ragú® Pizza Quick Sauce on bread slices, then top with mushroom mixture, cheese and basil. Bake 15 minutes or until heated through.

Makes 12 crostini

Recipe Tip: Many varieties of mushrooms are available in supermarkets and specialty grocery stores. Shiitake, portobello and cremini mushrooms all have excellent flavor.

Helpful Hint

Crostini, an Italian word meaning "little toasts," are usually made of small, thin slices of toasted bread that are brushed with olive oil.

Mushroom Parmesan Crostini

Wild Wedges

2 (8-inch) flour tortillas

Nonstick cooking spray

⅓ cup shredded Cheddar
cheese

⅓ cup chopped cooked
chicken or turkey

1 green onion, thinly sliced
(about ¼ cup)

2 tablespoons mild, thick and
chunky salsa

1. Heat large nonstick skillet over medium heat until hot.

2. Spray one side of one flour tortilla with nonstick cooking spray; place sprayed side down in skillet. Top with cheese, chicken, green onion and salsa. Place remaining tortilla over mixture; spray with nonstick cooking spray.

3. Cook 2 to 3 minutes per side or until golden brown and cheese is melted. Cut into 8 triangles. *Makes 4 servings*

Variation: For bean quesadillas, omit the chicken and spread ⅓ cup canned refried beans over one of the tortillas.

Beefy Stuffed Mushrooms

1 pound lean ground beef

2 teaspoons prepared
horseradish

1 teaspoon chopped chives

1 clove garlic, minced

¼ teaspoon black pepper

18 large mushrooms

⅔ cup dry white wine

1. Thoroughly mix ground beef, horseradish, chives, garlic and pepper in medium bowl.

2. Remove stems from mushrooms; stuff mushroom caps with beef mixture.

3. Place stuffed mushrooms in shallow baking dish; pour wine over mushrooms. Bake in preheated 350°F oven until meat is browned, about 20 minutes. *Makes 1½ dozen*

Wild Wedges

Smoked Chicken Bagel Snacks

⅓ cup cream cheese, softened

2 teaspoons spicy brown mustard

¼ cup chopped roasted red peppers

1 green onion with top, sliced

5 mini-bagels, split

3 ounces smoked chicken or turkey, cut into 10 very thin slices

¼ medium cucumber, cut into 10 thin slices

1. Combine cream cheese and mustard in small bowl; mix well. Stir in peppers and green onion.

2. Spread cream cheese mixture evenly onto cut sides of bagels. Cover bottom halves of bagels with chicken, folding chicken to fit onto bagels; top with cucumber slices and tops of bagels.

Makes 5 servings

Marinated Artichoke Cheese Toasts

1 jar (8 ounces) marinated artichoke hearts, drained

½ cup (2 ounces) shredded Swiss cheese

⅓ cup finely chopped roasted red peppers

⅓ cup finely chopped celery

1 tablespoon plus 1 ½ teaspoons mayonnaise

24 melba toast rounds

Paprika

1. Rinse artichokes under cold running water; drain well. Pat dry with paper towels. Finely chop artichokes; place in medium bowl. Add cheese, peppers, celery and mayonnaise; mix well.

2. Spoon artichoke mixture evenly onto melba toast rounds; place on large nonstick baking sheet or broiler pan. Broil, 6 inches from heat, about 45 seconds or until cheese mixture is hot and bubbly. Sprinkle with paprika. Garnish, if desired. *Makes 12 servings*

Smoked Chicken Bagel Snacks

Easy Sausage Empanadas

Prep Time: 25 minutes   **Cook Time:** 15 minutes

1 (15-ounce) package
   refrigerated pie crusts
   (2 crusts)

¼ pound bulk pork sausage

2 tablespoons finely chopped
   onion

⅛ teaspoon garlic powder

⅛ teaspoon ground cumin

⅛ teaspoon dried oregano,
   crushed

1 tablespoon chopped
   pimiento-stuffed olives

1 tablespoon chopped raisins

1 egg, separated

Let pie crusts stand at room temperature for 20 minutes or according to package directions. Crumble sausage into medium skillet. Add onion, garlic powder, cumin and oregano; cook over medium-high heat until sausage is no longer pink. Drain drippings. Stir in olives and raisins. Beat the egg yolk slightly; stir into sausage mixture, mixing well. Carefully unfold crusts. Cut into desired shapes using 3-inch cookie cutters. Place about 2 teaspoons of the sausage filling on half the cutouts. Top with remaining cutouts. Moisten fingers with water and pinch dough to seal edges. Slightly beat the egg white; gently brush over tops of empanadas. Bake in a 425°F oven 15 to 18 minutes or until golden brown.

Makes 12 appetizer servings

Favorite recipe from **National Pork Board**

Helpful Hint

Before chopping the raisins, spray your knife lightly with nonstick cooking spray to prevent them from sticking to the knife. For larger quantities of dried fruit, place the fruit in the freezer for an hour to make chopping easier.

Seafood Pinwheels

4 ounces light cream cheese

1 tablespoon thick and chunky picante sauce

7 flour tortillas (6-inch)

7 small leaves leaf lettuce, rough ends removed

1 (8-ounce) package surimi seafood, crab or lobster flavor, shredded

3 tablespoons sliced ripe olives

1 tablespoon minced cilantro

Additional picante sauce

Combine cream cheese and 1 tablespoon picante sauce in small mixing bowl; beat until smooth. Spread 1 tablespoon cream cheese mixture on each tortilla to within ½ inch of edge. Place lettuce leaf in center of each tortilla. Sprinkle 2 tablespoons surimi seafood in strip down center of lettuce leaf. Sprinkle with olives and cilantro. Roll up, jelly-roll style, as tightly as possible. Dampen edges of tortilla with a little water; press edges together to seal. Wrap each roll securely in plastic wrap; refrigerate at least 2 hours.

To serve, unwrap rolls. Trim ends; slice tortillas into 1-inch pieces. Serve with additional picante sauce. *Makes 35 servings*

*Favorite recipe from **National Fisheries Institute***

Mini Beef Tostadas

1 pound ground beef

1 tablespoon instant minced onion

1 can (8 ounces) refried beans

1 can (4 ounces) chopped green chilies, drained (optional)

½ cup bottled taco sauce

4 dozen round tortilla chips

1 cup (4 ounces) shredded Cheddar cheese

1. Cook and stir beef and onion in large skillet over medium heat about 10 minutes or until beef is no longer pink; drain and discard drippings.

2. Stir in beans, chilies and taco sauce; cook and stir until bubbly, about 4 minutes. Spoon about 1 heaping tablespoon beef mixture on top of each tortilla chip; sprinkle with cheese. Place on baking sheets.

3. Bake in preheated 375°F oven until cheese is melted, about 2 minutes. *Makes 4 dozen*

Spicy Apricot Sesame Wings

Prep Time: 15 minutes   **Marinate Time:** 20 minutes   **Cook Time:** 25 minutes

⅓ cup *Frank's*® *RedHot*® Cayenne Pepper Sauce

½ cup *French's*® Dijon Mustard

2 tablespoons Oriental sesame oil

1 tablespoon red wine vinegar

½ cup apricot jam

2 pounds chicken wings, split and tips discarded

2 tablespoons toasted sesame seeds*

To toast sesame seeds, place on baking sheet and bake at 375°F 8 to 10 minutes or until golden.

1. Stir *Frank's RedHot*, mustard, sesame oil and vinegar in small measuring cup. Spoon ¼ cup *Frank's RedHot* mixture and apricot jam into blender or food processor. Cover; process until smooth. Reserve for basting and dipping sauce.

2. Place wings in large bowl. Pour remaining *Frank's RedHot* mixture over wings; toss to coat. Cover; marinate in refrigerator 20 minutes.

3. Place wings on oiled grid and discard any remaining marinade. Grill over medium heat 25 to 30 minutes or until crispy and no longer pink, turning often. Brush with ¼ cup of the sauce during last 10 minutes of cooking. Place wings on serving platter; sprinkle with sesame seeds. Serve with remaining sauce.

Makes 8 servings

Spicy Apricot Sesame Wings

South-of-the-Border Quiche Squares

1 (8-ounce) package refrigerated crescent dinner roll dough

1½ cups shredded Monterey Jack and Colby cheese blend (6 ounces)

½ cup diced green chiles

½ cup chopped onion

4 eggs, beaten

1 cup milk

⅓ cup GREY POUPON® COUNTRY DIJON® Mustard

1 tablespoon chopped cilantro or parsley

½ teaspoon chili powder

Chopped tomato and yellow and green bell peppers, for garnish

Unroll dough and press perforations together. Press dough on bottom and 1 inch up sides of greased 13×9×2-inch baking pan. Bake crust at 375°F for 5 to 8 minutes or until lightly golden. Remove from oven; sprinkle with half the cheese. Top with chiles, onion and remaining cheese.

Blend eggs, milk, mustard, cilantro or parsley and chili powder in medium bowl. Pour mixture evenly over cheese layer. Bake at 375°F for 25 to 30 minutes or until set. Cool 5 minutes. Garnish with tomato and bell peppers; cut into 2-inch squares. Serve hot.

Makes 24 appetizers

Helpful Hint

To chop small amounts of fresh herbs, such as cilantro or parsley, quickly and easily, try using kitchen scissors instead of a knife.

South-of-the-Border Quiche Squares

Make-Ahead Munchies

Nicole's Cheddar Crisps

1¾ cups all-purpose flour

½ cup yellow cornmeal

½ teaspoon sugar

¾ teaspoon salt

¾ teaspoon baking soda

½ cup (1 stick) butter or margarine

1½ cups (6 ounces) shredded sharp Cheddar cheese

½ cup cold water

2 tablespoons white vinegar

Coarsely ground black pepper

Mix flour, cornmeal, sugar, salt and baking soda in large bowl. Cut in butter with pastry blender until mixture resembles coarse crumbs. Stir in cheese, water and vinegar with fork until mixture forms soft dough. Cover dough and refrigerate 1 hour or freeze 30 minutes until firm.

Preheat oven to 375°F. Grease 2 large cookie sheets. Divide dough into 4 pieces. Roll each piece into paper-thin circle (about 13 inches in diameter) on floured surface. Sprinkle with pepper; press pepper firmly into dough.

Cut each circle into 8 wedges; place wedges on prepared cookie sheets. Bake about 10 minutes or until crisp. Store in airtight container for up to 3 days.

Makes 32 crisps

Nicole's Cheddar Crisps

Creamy Pesto Dip

Prep Time: 5 minutes plus refrigerating

1 package (8 ounces) PHILADELPHIA® Cream Cheese, softened

3 tablespoons milk

⅓ cup DI GIORNO® Basil Pesto Sauce

1 red pepper, finely chopped (about 1 cup)

MIX cream cheese and milk with electric mixer on medium speed until smooth. Blend in pesto and red pepper. Refrigerate.

SERVE with assorted NABISCO® Crackers, cut-up vegetables, breadsticks or chips.

Makes about 2⅓ cups

Pinwheel Appetizers

1 (8-ounce) package fat-free cream cheese, softened

⅓ cup KNOTT'S® Jalapeño Jelly

1 (2-ounce) jar sliced pimientos, drained and chopped

5 burrito size fat-free flour tortillas

1 (4-ounce) can diced green chilies

1 (4.25-ounce) can chopped ripe olives

1 cup fat-free shredded Cheddar cheese

1. In medium mixing bowl, combine cream cheese, Knott's Jelly and pimientos; mix well.

2. On *each* flour tortilla, spread ⅓ cup filling. Evenly top *each* tortilla with green chilies, black olives, and cheese.

3. Tightly roll tortilla up in jelly-roll fashion. Wrap *each* roll in plastic wrap and refrigerate at least 1 hour.

4. To serve, remove plastic wrap and cut *each* tortilla roll into 1-inch slices.

Makes 35 to 40 pinwheels

Creamy Pesto Dip

Spiral Reuben Dijon Bites

1 sheet puff pastry
(½ package)

¼ cup GREY POUPON® Dijon
Mustard

6 slices Swiss cheese
(3 ounces)

6 slices deli corned beef
(6 ounces)

1 egg, beaten

1 tablespoon caraway seed

Additional GREY POUPON®
Dijon Mustard

Thaw puff pastry sheet according to package directions. Roll puff pastry dough to 12×10-inch rectangle. Spread mustard evenly over dough; top with cheese and corned beef. Cut in half crosswise to form 2 (10×6-inch) rectangles. Roll up each rectangle from short end, jelly-roll fashion; pinch seams to seal.*

Cut each roll into 16 (¼-inch-thick) slices. Place slices, cut-sides up, on lightly greased baking sheets; brush with beaten egg and sprinkle with caraway seed. Bake at 400°F for 10 to 12 minutes or until golden. Serve warm with additional mustard.

Makes 32 appetizers

*Rolls may be wrapped and frozen. To serve, thaw at room temperature for 30 minutes. Slice and bake as directed above.

Helpful Hint

Unused sheets of puff pastry should be wrapped in plastic wrap or foil and returned to the freezer. Try to handle puff pastry as little as possible to ensure tenderness. If the sheet of puff pastry becomes too soft while working with it, chill it in the refrigerator for a few minutes.

Spiral Reuben Dijon Bites

Cheese Twists

1 cup all-purpose flour

½ teaspoon baking soda

½ teaspoon dry mustard

½ teaspoon salt

⅛ teaspoon ground red pepper

¾ cup grated Parmesan cheese, divided

½ cup butter or margarine, softened

3 egg yolks

2 teaspoons water

1 egg white, slightly beaten

1 tablespoon sesame seeds (optional)

Preheat oven to 400°F. Grease two cookie sheets. Combine flour, baking soda, mustard, salt and red pepper in large bowl. Reserve 1 tablespoon cheese; stir remaining cheese into flour mixture. Cut in butter with pastry blender or 2 knives until mixture resembles fine crumbs. Add egg yolks and water, mixing until dough forms. Shape into a ball; flatten and wrap in plastic wrap. Refrigerate 2 hours or until firm.

Roll out dough on lightly floured surface into 12-inch square (about ⅛ inch thick). Brush surface lightly with egg white and sprinkle with remaining 1 tablespoon cheese and sesame seeds, if desired. Cut dough in half. Cut each half crosswise into ¼-inch strips. Twist 2 strips together. Repeat with remaining strips. Place 1 inch apart on prepared cookie sheets.

Bake 6 to 8 minutes or until light golden brown. Remove from cookie sheets and cool completely on wire racks. Store in airtight container. *Makes about 48 twists*

Variation: Prepare dough and cut as directed. Place ¾ of strips on cookie sheets. Form rings with remaining strips; seal edges. Place on cookie sheets. Bake and cool as directed. To serve, arrange 3 to 4 strips into small stacks. Insert stacks into rings.

Ortega® Green Chile Guacamole

2 medium very ripe
   avocados, seeded,
   peeled and mashed

1 can (4 ounces) ORTEGA®
   Diced Green Chiles

2 large green onions,
   chopped

2 tablespoons olive oil

1 teaspoon lime juice

1 clove garlic, finely chopped

¼ teaspoon salt

   Tortilla chips

COMBINE avocados, chiles, green onions, olive oil, lime juice, garlic and salt in medium bowl. Cover; refrigerate for at least 1 hour. Serve with chips. *Makes 2 cups*

Tip: This all-time favorite dip can be used in tacos, burritos, tamales, chimichangas or combined with Ortega® Salsa Prima™ for a spicy salad dressing.

Creamy Roasted Red Pepper Dip

Prep Time: 5 minutes plus refrigerating

1 package (8 ounces)
   PHILADELPHIA® Cream
   Cheese, softened

3 tablespoons milk

½ cup chopped, drained
   roasted red peppers

½ teaspoon dried thyme
   leaves

⅛ teaspoon ground black
   pepper

MIX cream cheese and milk with electric mixer on medium speed until smooth. Blend in remaining ingredients. Refrigerate.

SERVE with NABISCO® Crackers or assorted cut-up vegetables.

Makes 1½ cups

Easy Spinach Appetizer

2 tablespoons butter

3 eggs

1 cup milk

1 cup all-purpose flour

1 teaspoon baking powder

1 teaspoon salt

4 cups (16 ounces) shredded Monterey Jack cheese

2 packages (10 ounces each) frozen chopped spinach, thawed and well drained

½ cup diced red bell pepper

Preheat oven to 350°F. Melt butter in 13×9-inch pan.

Beat eggs, milk, flour, milk, baking powder and salt in medium bowl until blended. Stir in cheese, spinach and bell pepper; mix well. Spread mixture over melted butter in pan.

Bake 40 to 45 minutes or until firm. Let stand 10 minures before cutting into triangles or squares. *Makes 2 to 4 dozen pieces*

Tip: Easy Spinach Appetizer may be made ahead, frozen and reheated. After baking, cool completely and cut into squares. Transfer squares to cookie sheet; place cookie sheet in freezer until squares are frozen solid. Transfer to resealable plastic food storage bag. To serve, reheat squares in 325°F oven for 15 minutes.

Chunky Hawaiian Spread

1 package (3 ounces) light cream cheese, softened

½ cup fat free or light sour cream

1 can (8 ounces) DOLE® Crushed Pineapple, well-drained

¼ cup mango chutney*

Low fat crackers

If there are large pieces of fruit in chutney, cut into small pieces.

• Beat cream cheese, sour cream, pineapple and chutney in bowl until blended. Cover and chill 1 hour or overnight. Serve with crackers. Refrigerate any leftover spread in airtight container for up to one week. *Makes 2½ cups*

Easy Spinach Appetizer

Rice & Artichoke Phyllo Triangles

1 box UNCLE BEN'S® Butter &
  Herb Fast Cook Recipe
  Long Grain & Wild Rice

1 jar (6½ ounces) marinated
  quartered artichokes,
  drained and finely
  chopped

2 tablespoons grated
  Parmesan cheese

1 tablespoon minced onion
  or 1 green onion with
  top, finely chopped

⅓ cup plain yogurt or sour
  cream

10 sheets frozen phyllo dough,
  thawed

1. Prepare rice according to package directions. Cool completely.

2. Preheat oven to 375°F. In medium bowl, combine rice, artichokes, Parmesan cheese and onion; mix well. Stir in yogurt until well blended.

3. Place one sheet of phyllo dough on a damp kitchen towel. (Keep remaining dough covered.) Lightly spray dough with nonstick cooking spray. Fold dough in half by bringing short sides of dough together; spray lightly with additional cooking spray.

4. Cut dough into four equal strips, each about 3¼ inches wide. For each appetizer, spoon about 1 tablespoon rice mixture onto dough about 1 inch from end of each strip. Fold 1 corner over filling to make triangle. Continue folding as you would fold a flag to form a triangle that encloses filling. Repeat with remaining dough and filling.

5. Place triangles on greased baking sheets. Spray triangles with nonstick cooking spray. Bake 12 to 15 minutes or until golden brown. *Makes 40 appetizers*

Cook's Tips: To simplify preparation, the rice mixture can be prepared a day ahead, covered and refrigerated until ready to use. Use a pizza cutter to cut phyllo dough into strips.

Southwestern Chili Cheese Empanadas

Make-Ahead Time: up to 2 months in freezer   **Final Prep Time:** 30 minutes

¾ **cup (3 ounces) finely shredded taco-flavored cheese***

⅓ **cup diced green chiles, drained**

1 package (15 ounces) refrigerated pie crusts

1 egg

Chili powder

*If taco-flavored cheese is unavailable, toss ¾ cup shredded marbled Monterey Jack cheese with ½ teaspoon chili powder.

1. Combine cheese and chiles in small bowl.

2. Unfold 1 pastry crust on floured surface. Roll into 13-inch circle. Cut dough into 16 rounds using 3-inch cookie cutter, rerolling scraps as necessary. Repeat with remaining crust to total 32 circles.

3. Spoon 1 teaspoon cheese mixture in center of each dough round. Fold round in half, sealing edge with tines of fork.

4. Place empanadas on wax paper-lined baking sheets; freeze, uncovered, 1 hour or until firm. Place in resealable plastic food storage bags. Freeze up to 2 months.

5. To complete recipe, preheat oven to 400°F. Place frozen empanadas on ungreased baking sheet. Beat egg and 1 tablespoon water in small bowl; brush on empanadas. Sprinkle with chili powder.

6. Bake 12 to 17 minutes or until golden brown. Remove from baking sheet to wire rack to cool.   *Makes 32 appetizers*

Serving suggestion: Serve empanadas with salsa and sour cream.

Beef Tortilla Spirals

1 (8-ounce) package cream cheese, softened

½ cup A.1.® Original or A.1.® BOLD & SPICY Steak Sauce

¼ cup chopped green onions

2 teaspoons prepared horseradish

6 (10-inch) flour tortillas

2 cups fresh spinach leaves

18 ounces deli-sliced roast beef

6 ounces deli-sliced provolone cheese, optional

½ red bell pepper, cut into julienne strips

½ yellow bell pepper, cut into julienne strips

½ green bell pepper, cut into julienne strips

In small bowl, with electric mixer at medium speed, blend cream cheese, steak sauce, green onions and horseradish until smooth. On each tortilla, spread 2 tablespoons cream cheese mixture. Top each with a single layer of spinach leaves, 3 ounces roast beef and 1 ounce provolone if desired. Spread with 1 tablespoon cream cheese mixture. Place red, yellow and green pepper strips near one end of each tortilla, dividing evenly; roll up jelly-roll fashion.

Wrap tightly in plastic wrap; refrigerate several hours or overnight. To serve, cut each roll into 8 slices. *Makes 48 appetizers*

Roasted Pepper & Tomato Salsa

3 yellow or red bell peppers

2 poblano peppers

1 large onion

4 cloves garlic, minced

2 tablespoons olive oil

1 teaspoon dried oregano
  leaves

¾ teaspoon salt

½ teaspoon black pepper

2 cans (14 ½ ounces each)
  diced tomatoes

¾ cup tomato juice

¼ cup chopped fresh cilantro

1 tablespoon lime juice

1. Preheat oven to 350°F. Chop peppers and onion into ¾-inch pieces. Combine peppers, onion, garlic, olive oil, oregano, salt and black pepper in large bowl; toss to coat. Spread onto two 15×10×1-inch baking pans. Bake 20 minutes or until peppers and onion are lightly browned, stirring after 10 minutes.

2. Combine roasted vegetables and remaining ingredients in large bowl. Store in refrigerator up to 10 days or freeze up to 2 months.

Makes 6 cups

Fiery Garlic Bagel Thins

5 bagels

½ cup (1 stick) butter

6 cloves garlic, minced

2 tablespoons lemon juice

½ teaspoon TABASCO® brand
  Pepper Sauce

Salt to taste

Preheat broiler. Slice bagels crosswise into fifths. Melt butter in small saucepan. Add garlic; cook over low heat for 2 minutes or until garlic has softened. Add lemon juice, TABASCO® Sauce and salt. Liberally brush one side of each bagel slice with lemon-garlic butter. Broil bagels on one side until golden. (Watch carefully; this only takes a minute.) Turn bagels over and broil until golden. Serve hot or store in an airtight container.

Makes 25 bagel thins

Roasted Pepper & Tomato Salsa

Celebration Cheese Ball

2 packages (8 ounces) cream cheese, softened

⅓ cup mayonnaise

¼ cup grated Parmesan cheese

2 tablespoons finely chopped carrot

1 tablespoon finely chopped red onion

1½ teaspoons prepared horseradish

¼ teaspoon salt

½ cup chopped pecans or walnuts

Assorted crackers and breadsticks

Blend all ingredients except pecans and crackers in medium bowl. Cover and refrigerate until firm.

Form cheese mixture into a ball; roll in pecans. Wrap cheese ball in plastic wrap and refrigerate at least 1 hour. Serve with assorted crackers and breadsticks.

Makes about 2⅔ cups

Creamy Garlic Salsa Dip

1 envelope LIPTON® RECIPE SECRETS® Savory Herb with Garlic Soup Mix*

1 container (16 ounces) sour cream

½ cup your favorite prepared salsa

Also terrific with LIPTON® RECIPE SECRETS® Onion Soup Mix.

1. In medium bowl, combine all ingredients; chill at least 2 hours.

2. Serve with your favorite dippers.

Makes 2½ cups dip

Celebration Cheese Ball

Black Bean Spirals

Prep Time: 15 minutes plus refrigerating

1 can (15 ounces) black beans, rinsed, drained

6 flour tortillas (10-inch)

1 package (8 ounces) PHILADELPHIA® Cream Cheese, softened

1 cup KRAFT® Shredded Cheddar *or* Monterey Jack Cheese

½ cup BREAKSTONE'S® or KNUDSEN® Sour Cream

¼ teaspoon onion salt

TACO BELL® HOME ORIGINALS® Thick 'N Chunky Salsa

PLACE beans in food processor container fitted with steel blade or blender container; cover. Process until smooth. Spread layer of beans on each tortilla.

PLACE cheeses, sour cream and onion salt in food processor container fitted with steel blade or blender container; cover. Process until smooth. Spread cheese mixture over beans.

ROLL tortillas up tightly. Refrigerate 30 minutes. Cut into ½-inch slices. Serve TACO BELL® HOME ORIGINALS® Thick 'N Chunky Salsa.

Makes 20 servings

Great Substitute: Substitute 1 can (16 ounces) TACO BELL® HOME ORIGINALS® Refried Beans for puréed black beans.

Helpful Hint

Black Bean Spirals can be made a few hours or up to 24 hours ahead of time. Keep them in the refrigerator and cut them just before serving.

Black Bean Spirals

Tangy Wisconsin Blue Cheese Whip

Prep Time: 15 minutes

1 cup whipping cream

½ cup finely crumbled
Wisconsin Blue cheese
(2 ounces)

1 teaspoon dried basil,
crushed

¼ teaspoon garlic salt

½ cup almonds, toasted and
chopped

Assorted vegetable or fruit
dippers

In a small mixer bowl combine whipping cream, Blue cheese, basil and garlic salt. Beat with an electric mixer on medium speed until slightly thickened. Gently fold in chopped almonds. Serve with vegetable or fruit dippers. (Dip can be made ahead and chilled, covered, up to 2 hours.) *Makes about 2 cups*

Favorite recipe from **Wisconsin Milk Marketing Board**

Orange Dijon Chicken Wings

½ cup GREY POUPON®
COUNTRY DIJON®
Mustard

½ cup ketchup

⅓ cup orange marmalade

1 tablespoon reduced-sodium
soy sauce

1 tablespoon dried minced
onion

1 clove garlic, crushed

12 chicken wings, split and
tips removed

Blend mustard, ketchup, marmalade, soy sauce, onion and garlic in small bowl. Place chicken wings in plastic bag; coat with ½ cup mustard mixture. Refrigerate chicken wings and remaining mustard mixture for at least 1 hour.

Place chicken wings on baking sheet. Bake at 375°F for 20 minutes, pouring off any excess fat. Bake 20 to 25 minutes more or until done. Heat remaining mustard mixture until warm; serve as dipping sauce with hot wings. *Makes 24 appetizers*

Spinach Quiches

1 package (15 ounces)
   refrigerated pie crust or
   pastry for double-crust
   (10-inch) pie

2 teaspoons vegetable oil

¼ cup finely chopped
   mushrooms

2 tablespoons finely chopped
   onion

1 clove garlic, minced

1 cup frozen chopped
   spinach, thawed and
   squeezed dry

1 teaspoon dried oregano
   leaves

½ teaspoon dried mint leaves

½ cup ricotta cheese or small
   curd cottage cheese

2 tablespoons all-purpose
   flour

¾ teaspoon salt

⅛ teaspoon white pepper

2 eggs

2 tablespoons reduced-fat
   (2%) milk

1. Preheat oven to 400°F. Roll 1 pie crust on lightly floured surface into circle ⅛ inch thick. Cut into 18 circles with 1½-inch cutter. Ease pastries into mini-muffin tins; flute edges with tines of fork. Repeat with remaining pie crust. Bake 8 to 10 minutes or until pastry shells are lightly browned; cool.

2. *Reduce heat to 325°F.* Heat oil in medium saucepan over medium heat until hot. Add mushrooms, onion and garlic; cook and stir 2 to 3 minutes or until onion is tender. Stir in spinach, oregano and mint; cook 5 minutes, stirring occasionally, or until no excess moisture remains. Remove from heat.

3. Stir ricotta cheese and remaining ingredients into spinach mixture. Spoon 2 teaspoons mixture into each prepared pastry shell. Bake 20 to 25 minutes or until set and tops are lightly browned. Cool quiches completely. Cover and refrigerate up to 1 day or freeze up to 1 month.

4. To complete recipe, preheat oven to 325°F. Bake 10 minutes or until hot. (If frozen, allow at least 4 hours to defrost in refrigerator.)

Makes 36 servings

Stuffed Party Baguette

2 medium red bell peppers

1 French bread loaf, about 14 inches long

¼ cup plus 2 tablespoons prepared Italian dressing, divided

1 small red onion, very thinly sliced

8 large fresh basil leaves

3 ounces Swiss cheese, very thinly sliced

1. Preheat oven to 425°F. Cover large baking sheet with foil.

2. To roast bell peppers, cut peppers in half; remove stems, seeds and membranes. Place peppers, cut sides down, on prepared baking sheet. Bake 20 to 25 minutes or until skins are browned, turning occasionally.

3. Transfer peppers from baking sheet to paper bag; close bag tightly. Let stand 10 minutes or until peppers are cool enough to handle and skins are loosened. Peel off skins using sharp knife; discard skins. Cut peppers into strips.

4. Trim ends from bread; discard ends. Cut loaf lengthwise in half. Remove soft insides of loaf; reserve removed bread for another use.

5. Brush ¼ cup Italian dressing evenly onto cut sides of bread. Arrange pepper strips in even layer in bottom half of loaf; top with even layer of onion. Brush onion with remaining 2 tablespoons Italian dressing; top with layer of basil and cheese. Replace bread top. Wrap loaf tightly in heavy-duty plastic wrap; refrigerate at least 2 hours or overnight.

6. When ready to serve, cut loaf crosswise into 1-inch slices. Secure with wooden picks and garnish, if desired.   *Makes 12 servings*

Stuffed Party Baguette

Mini Crab Cakes

1 pound crabmeat

1 cup fine, dry bread crumbs, divided

2 eggs, beaten

¼ cup minced onion

¼ cup minced green bell pepper

¼ cup minced red bell pepper

1 teaspoon dry mustard

½ teaspoon TABASCO® brand Pepper Sauce

Salt to taste

Vegetable oil

Zesty Remoulade Sauce (page 198)

Fresh herbs (optional)

Combine crabmeat, ½ cup bread crumbs, eggs, onion, bell peppers, mustard, TABASCO® Sauce and salt in large bowl. Cover and refrigerate 1 to 2 hours or until mixture becomes firm. Shape mixture into small cakes, about 1×1½ inches. Coat cakes in remaining ½ cup bread crumbs.

Pour oil into heavy skillet to depth of ⅓ inch; heat skillet over medium heat. When oil is hot, cook crab cakes about 3 to 5 minutes on each side or until browned. Remove to paper towels. Serve crab cakes warm; top with dollops of Zesty Remoulade Sauce. Garnish with herbs, if desired. *Makes 20 to 25 cakes*

Helpful Hint

Remoulade sauce is a classic French sauce that traditionally combines mayonnaise, mustard, gherkins, capers, herbs and anchovies. There are numerous variations of the sauce, which is often served (chilled) with fish and shellfish.

Mini Crab Cakes

Mexicali Appetizer Meatballs

⅔ cup A.1.® Steak Sauce

⅔ cup thick and chunky salsa

1½ pounds ground beef

1 egg

½ cup plain dry bread crumbs

Blend steak sauce and salsa in small bowl. Mix ground beef, egg, bread crumbs and ⅓ cup sauce mixture in separate bowl; shape into 32 (1¼-inch) meatballs. Arrange meatballs in single layer in shallow baking pan.

Bake at 425°F for 12 to 15 minutes or until meatballs are cooked through. Serve hot meatballs with remaining sauce mixture as a dip.

Makes 32 (1¼-inch) meatballs

Zesty Remoulade Sauce

1 cup mayonnaise

2 to 3 green onions, finely chopped

1 celery stalk, finely chopped

2 tablespoons prepared horseradish, drained

1 tablespoon finely chopped chives

1 tablespoon Dijon mustard

1 tablespoon fresh lemon juice

1 clove garlic, finely chopped

½ teaspoon TABASCO® brand Pepper Sauce

Combine all ingredients in medium bowl. Cover and refrigerate 1 hour to blend flavors. Serve chilled.

Makes 1¾ cups

Veg•All® Quiche Squares

1 package (12 ounces) frozen pie crusts, thawed

1 can (15 ounces) VEG•ALL® Original Mixed Vegetables, drained

1 cup shredded Swiss cheese

8 slices cooked bacon, crumbled

6 eggs

1 cup milk

1 tablespoon minced onion

¼ teaspoon seasoned salt

⅛ to ¼ teaspoon ground nutmeg

Preheat oven to 350°F. Line 9×13-inch pan with pie crusts. Sprinkle Veg•All, cheese and bacon over crust. In medium mixing bowl, beat together remaining ingredients; pour into pan. Bake for 35 minutes or until knife inserted in center comes out clean. Cool 5 minutes before cutting.

Makes 24 squares

Roasted Garlic Spread with Three Cheeses

2 medium heads garlic

2 packages (8 ounces each) cream cheese, softened

1 package (3½ ounces) goat cheese

2 tablespoons (1 ounce) crumbled blue cheese

1 teaspoon dried thyme leaves

1. Preheat oven to 400°F. Cut tops off garlic heads to expose tops of cloves. Place garlic in small baking pan; bake 45 minutes or until garlic is very tender. Remove from pan; cool completely. Squeeze garlic into small bowl; mash with fork.

2. Beat cream cheese and goat cheese in small bowl until smooth; stir in blue cheese, garlic and thyme. Cover; refrigerate 3 hours or overnight. Spoon dip into serving bowl; serve with cucumbers, radishes, carrots, yellow bell peppers or crackers, if desired.

Makes 2½ cups

Hidden Valley® Bacon-Cheddar Ranch Dip

1 container (16 ounces) sour cream (2 cups)

1 packet (1 ounce) HIDDEN VALLEY® Original Ranch® Dips Mix

1 cup (4 ounces) shredded Cheddar cheese

¼ cup crisp-cooked, crumbled bacon*

Potato chips or corn chips, for dipping

*Bacon pieces may be used.

Combine sour cream and dips mix. Stir in cheese and bacon. Chill at least 1 hour. Serve with chips.   *Makes about 3 cups*

Picante Vegetable Dip

⅔ cup reduced-fat sour cream

½ cup picante sauce

⅓ cup mayonnaise or reduced-fat mayonnaise

¼ cup finely chopped green or red bell pepper

2 tablespoons finely chopped green onion

¾ teaspoon garlic salt

Assorted fresh vegetable dippers or tortilla chips

Combine sour cream, picante sauce, mayonnaise, bell pepper, green onion and garlic salt in medium bowl until well blended. Cover; refrigerate several hours or overnight to allow flavors to blend. Serve with dippers.   *Makes about 1⅔ cups*

Hidden Valley® Bacon-Cheddar Ranch Dip

Antipasto Crescent Bites

2 ounces cream cheese (do not use reduced-fat or fat-free cream cheese)

1 package (8 ounces) refrigerated crescent roll dough

1 egg plus 1 tablespoon water, beaten

4 strips roasted red pepper, cut into 3×¾-inch-long strips

2 large marinated artichoke hearts, cut in half lengthwise to ¾-inch width

1 thin slice Genoa or other salami, cut into 4 strips

4 small stuffed green olives, cut into halves

1. Preheat oven to 375°F. Cut cream cheese into 16 equal pieces, about 1 teaspoon per piece; set aside.

2. Remove dough from package. Unroll on lightly floured surface. Cut each triangle of dough in half to form 2 triangles. Brush outer edges of triangle lightly with egg mixture.

3. Wrap 1 pepper strip around 1 piece of cream cheese. Place on dough triangle. Fold over and pinch edges to seal; repeat with remaining pepper strips. Place 1 piece artichoke heart and 1 piece of cream cheese on dough triangle. Fold over and pinch edges to seal; repeat with remaining pieces of artichoke hearts. Wrap 1 strip salami around 1 piece of cream cheese. Place on dough triangle. Fold over and pinch edges to seal; repeat with remaining salami. Place 2 olive halves and 1 piece of cream cheese on dough triangle. Fold over and pinch edges to seal; repeat with remaining olives. Place evenly spaced on ungreased baking sheet. Brush with egg mixture.

4. Bake 12 to 14 minutes or until golden brown. Cool on wire rack. Store in airtight container in refrigerator.

5. Reheat on baking sheet in preheated 325°F oven 7 to 8 minutes or until warmed through. Do not microwave.

Makes 16 pieces

Angelic Deviled Eggs

6 large eggs

¼ cup cottage cheese

3 tablespoons prepared ranch dressing

2 teaspoons Dijon mustard

2 tablespoons minced fresh chives or dill

1 tablespoon diced well-drained pimiento or roasted red pepper

1. Place eggs in medium saucepan; add enough water to cover. Bring to a boil over medium heat. Remove from heat; cover. Let stand 20 minutes. Drain. Add cold water to eggs in saucepan; let stand until eggs are cool. Drain. Remove shells from eggs.

2. Cut eggs lengthwise in half. Remove yolks, reserving 3 yolk halves. Discard remaining yolks or reserve for another use. Place egg whites, cut sides up, on serving plate; cover with plastic wrap. Refrigerate while preparing filling.

3. Combine cottage cheese, dressing, mustard and reserved yolk halves in mini food processor; process until smooth. (Or, place in small bowl and mash with fork until well blended.) Transfer cheese mixture to small bowl; stir in chives and pimiento. Spoon into egg whites. Cover and chill at least 1 hour. Garnish, if desired. *Makes 12 servings*

Helpful Hint

Letting hard-boiled eggs cool in cold water or ice water after cooking prevents a dark grayish-green surface from forming on the yolks.

Polenta Triangles

3 cups cold water

1 cup yellow cornmeal

1 envelope LIPTON® RECIPE SECRETS® Golden Onion or Onion Soup Mix

1 can (4 ounces) mild chopped green chilies, drained

½ cup thawed frozen or drained canned whole kernel corn

⅓ cup finely chopped roasted red peppers

½ cup shredded sharp cheddar cheese (about 2 ounces)

In 3-quart saucepan, bring water to a boil over high heat. With wire whisk, stir in cornmeal, then golden onion soup mix. Reduce heat to low and simmer uncovered, stirring constantly, 25 minutes or until thickened. Stir in chilies, corn and roasted red peppers.

Spread into lightly greased 9-inch square baking pan; sprinkle with cheese. Let stand 20 minutes or until firm; cut into triangles. Serve at room temperature or heat in oven at 350° for 5 minutes or until warm.

Makes about 24 triangles

Raspberry Mushroom Kabobs

1 pound button mushrooms

1 cup (12-ounce jar) SMUCKER'S® Red Raspberry Preserves

½ cup red wine vinegar

1 teaspoon mustard

1 clove garlic, minced

1 tablespoon chopped parsley

Salt and pepper, to taste

Remove mushroom stems and reserve for another use. Blanch mushroom caps in boiling salted water for 5 minutes.

Dissolve preserves in red wine vinegar. Stir in mustard, garlic, parsley, salt and pepper. Drain cooked mushrooms and add to sauce to cool. (Recipe can be prepared to this point up to 3 days in advance.) Thread 3 to 4 mushrooms on each of 12 skewers. Place skewers on preheated grill. Cook for 3 minutes on each side before serving.

Makes 12 kabobs

Tortellini Kabobs with Pesto Ranch Dip

Prep and Cook Time: 30 minutes

½ **bag (16 ounces) frozen tortellini**

1¼ **cups ranch salad dressing**

½ **cup grated Parmesan cheese**

3 **cloves garlic, minced**

2 **teaspoons dried basil leaves**

1. Cook tortellini according to package directions. Rinse and drain under cold water. Thread tortellini onto bamboo skewers, 2 tortellini per skewer.

2. Combine salad dressing, cheese, garlic and basil in small bowl. Serve tortellini kabobs with dip. *Makes 6 to 8 servings*

Serving suggestion: For an even quicker dip, combine purchased spaghetti sauce or salsa with some finely chopped black olives.

Sausage Pinwheels

2 **cups biscuit mix**

½ **cup milk**

¼ **cup butter or margarine, melted**

1 **pound BOB EVANS® Original Recipe Roll Sausage**

Combine biscuit mix, milk and butter in large bowl until blended. Refrigerate 30 minutes. Divide dough into two portions. Roll out one portion on floured surface to ⅛-inch-thick rectangle, about 10×7 inches. Spread with half the sausage. Roll lengthwise into long roll. Repeat with remaining dough and sausage. Place rolls in freezer until hard enough to cut easily. Preheat oven to 400°F. Cut rolls into thin slices. Place on baking sheets. Bake 15 minutes or until golden brown. Serve hot. Refrigerate leftovers. *Makes 48 appetizers*

Note: This recipe may be doubled. Refreeze after slicing. When ready to serve, thaw slices in refrigerator and bake.

Tortellini Kabobs with Pesto Ranch Dip

Nutty Bacon Cheeseball

1 package (8 ounces) cream cheese, softened

½ cup milk

2 cups (8 ounces) shredded sharp Cheddar cheese

2 cups (8 ounces) shredded Monterey Jack cheese

¼ cup (1 ounce) crumbled blue cheese

¼ cup finely minced green onions (white parts only)

1 jar (2 ounces) diced pimento, drained

10 slices bacon, cooked, drained, finely crumbled and divided

¾ cup finely chopped pecans, divided

Salt and black pepper to taste

¼ cup minced parsley

1 tablespoon poppy seeds

Beat cream cheese and milk on low speed in large bowl with electric mixer until blended. Add cheeses. Blend on medium speed until well combined. Add green onions, pimento, half of bacon and half of pecans. Blend on medium speed until well mixed. Add salt and pepper to taste. Transfer half of mixture to large piece of plastic wrap. Form into ball; wrap tightly. Repeat with remaining mixture. Refrigerate until chilled, at least two hours.

Combine remaining bacon and pecans with parsley and poppy seeds in pie plate or large dinner plate. Remove plastic wrap from each ball; roll each in bacon mixture until well coated. Wrap each ball tightly in plastic wrap and refrigerate until ready to use, up to 24 hours. *Makes about 24 servings*

Nutty Bacon Cheeseball

Chicken Empanadas

1 box (15 ounces)
    refrigerated pie crusts
    (two 11-inch rounds)

4 ounces cream cheese

2 tablespoons salsa

2 tablespoons chopped fresh
    cilantro

½ teaspoon ground cumin

½ teaspoon salt

¼ teaspoon garlic powder

1 cup finely chopped cooked
    chicken

1 egg, beaten

    Additional salsa

Remove pie crust pouches from box; let stand at room temperature 15 to 20 minutes.

Heat cream cheese in small heavy saucepan over low heat; cook and stir until melted. Add salsa, cilantro, cumin, salt and garlic powder; stir until smooth. Stir in chicken; remove from heat.

Unfold pie crusts; remove plastic film. Roll out slightly on lightly floured surface. Cut crusts into 3-inch rounds using biscuit cutter or drinking glass. Reroll pie crust scraps to equal 20 rounds.

Preheat oven to 425°F. Place about 2 teaspoons chicken mixture in center of each round. Brush edges lightly with water. Pull one side of dough over filling to form half circle; pinch edges to seal.

Place 10 to 12 empanadas on foil-lined baking sheet; brush lightly with egg. Bake 16 to 18 minutes or until lightly brown. Serve with salsa.   *Makes 10 appetizer servings*

Note: Empanadas can be prepared ahead of time and frozen. Simply wrap unbaked empanadas with plastic wrap and freeze. To bake, follow directions baking 18 to 20 minutes.

Savory Quiche Squares

4 eggs

½ cup milk

½ cup Parmesan cheese

1 teaspoon LAWRY'S® Seasoned Salt

1 teaspoon LAWRY'S® Seasoned Pepper

½ teaspoon LAWRY'S® Garlic Powder with Parsley

2 teaspoons butter

¼ cup dry bread crumbs

1 cup (4 ounces) shredded Swiss cheese

½ cup chopped green onion, including tops

1 large tomato, seeded and diced

2 cups (8 ounces) shredded Monterey Jack cheese

In large bowl, beat together eggs and milk. Add Parmesan cheese, Seasoned Salt, Seasoned Pepper and Garlic Powder with Parsley; mix well and set aside. Grease an 8-inch square baking dish with butter; sprinkle evenly with bread crumbs. Top (in layers) with Swiss cheese, onion, tomato and Monterey Jack cheese. Pour egg mixture over. Bake, uncovered, in 350°F oven 25 to 30 minutes or until center is set. Cool on rack. *Makes 6 main dish or 20 appetizer servings*

Serving Suggestion: Cut into squares. Serve warm or chilled.

Hint: Cooking spray can be used in place of butter to grease dish.

The Famous Lipton® California Dip

1 envelope LIPTON® RECIPE
  SECRETS® Onion Soup
  Mix

1 container (16 ounces)
  regular or light sour
  cream

1. In medium bowl, blend all ingredients; chill at least 2 hours.

2. Serve with your favorite dippers.   *Makes about 2 cups dip*

Tip: For a creamier dip, add more sour cream.

Sensational Spinach Dip: Add 1 package (10 ounces) frozen chopped spinach, thawed and squeezed dry.

California Seafood Dip: Add 1 cup finely chopped cooked clams, crabmeat or shrimp, ¼ cup chili sauce and 1 tablespoon horseradish.

California Bacon Dip: Add ⅓ cup crumbled cooked bacon or bacon bits.

California Blue Cheese Dip: Add ¼ pound crumbled blue cheese and ¼ cup finely chopped walnuts.

The Famous Lipton® California Dip

Chile 'n' Cheese Spirals

4 ounces cream cheese,
    softened

1 cup (4 ounces) shredded
    Cheddar cheese

1 can (4 ounces) ORTEGA®
    Diced Green Chiles

3 green onions, sliced

1 can (2.25 ounces)
    chopped ripe olives

4 (8-inch) soft taco-size flour
    tortillas

ORTEGA® SALSA PRIMA™
    Garden Style

COMBINE cream cheese, Cheddar cheese, chiles, green onions and olives in medium bowl.

SPREAD ½ cup cheese mixture on each tortilla; roll up. Wrap each roll in plastic wrap; chill for 1 hour.

REMOVE plastic wrap; slice each roll into six ¾-inch pieces. Serve with salsa for dipping.   *Makes 24 appetizers*

Tip: Chili 'n' Cheese Spirals can be made ahead and kept in the refrigerator for 1 to 2 days. For added variety, add diced red bell pepper or use whole green chiles instead of diced.

Helpful Hint

Even the simplest appetizers can impress your guests when they're presented with flair. If you don't have traditional serving platters, you can use wooden cutting boards, unusual trays, baskets, mirrors or small plates. If a dish needs color, brighten it up with festive napkins, fresh herbs, fruit or flowers arranged around the plate.

Chile 'n' Cheese Spirals

Chinatown Stuffed Mushrooms

24 large fresh mushrooms (about 1 pound), cleaned and stems trimmed

½ pound ground turkey

1 clove garlic, minced

¼ cup fine dry bread crumbs

¼ cup thinly sliced green onions

3 tablespoons reduced-sodium soy sauce, divided

1 teaspoon minced fresh ginger

1 egg white, slightly beaten

⅛ teaspoon red pepper flakes (optional)

Remove stems from mushrooms; finely chop enough stems to equal 1 cup. Cook turkey with chopped stems and garlic in medium skillet over medium-high heat until turkey is no longer pink, stirring to separate turkey. Spoon off any fat. Stir in bread crumbs, green onions, 2 tablespoons soy sauce, ginger, egg white and pepper flakes, if desired; mix well.

Brush mushroom caps lightly on all sides with remaining 1 tablespoon soy sauce; spoon about 2 teaspoons stuffing into each mushroom cap.* Place stuffed mushrooms on rack of foil-lined broiler pan. Broil 4 to 5 inches from heat 5 to 6 minutes or until hot.

Makes 24 appetizers

Mushrooms may be made ahead to this point; cover and refrigerate up to 24 hours. Add 1 to 2 minutes to broiling time for chilled mushrooms.

Corned Beef & Swiss Appetizers

Prep Time: 20 minutes   **Broil Time:** 3 minutes

1 package (8 ounces) PHILADELPHIA® Cream Cheese, softened

2 teaspoons Grey Poupon® Dijon Mustard

¼ pound corned beef, chopped

½ cup (2 ounces) KRAFT® Shredded Swiss Cheese

2 tablespoons chopped green onion

36 slices cocktail rye bread, toasted

MIX cream cheese and mustard with electric mixer on medium speed until smooth.

BLEND in meat, Swiss cheese and onion. Spread on toast slices. Place on cookie sheet.

BROIL 2 to 3 minutes or until lightly browned.   *Makes 3 dozen*

To Make Ahead: Prepare as directed except for broiling. Place on cookie sheet. Freeze 1 hour or until firm. Place in freezer-safe zipper-style plastic bags. Freeze up to 1 month. When ready to serve, thaw 10 minutes. Broil as directed.

Global Flavors

Tortilla Pizzettes

1 cup chunky salsa

1 cup refried beans

2 tablespoons chopped fresh cilantro

½ teaspoon ground cumin

3 large (10-inch) flour tortillas

1 cup (4 ounces) shredded Mexican cheese blend

Pour salsa into strainer; let drain at least 20 minutes.

Meanwhile, combine refried beans, cilantro and cumin in small bowl; mix well. Preheat oven to 400°F. Spray baking sheet lightly with nonstick cooking spray; set aside.

Cut each tortilla into 2½-inch circles with round cookie cutter (9 to 10 circles per tortilla). Spread each tortilla circle with refried bean mixture, leaving ¼ inch around edge. Top with heaping teaspoon drained salsa; sprinkle with about 1 teaspoon cheese.

Place pizzettes on prepared baking sheet. Bake about 7 minutes or until tortillas are golden brown.   *Makes about 30 pizzettes*

Tortilla Pizzettes

Thai Chicken Skewers

¼ cup smooth peanut butter

2 tablespoons finely chopped onion

2 tablespoons finely chopped parsley

2 tablespoons fresh lemon juice

1 ½ teaspoons soy sauce

1 clove garlic, finely chopped

1 teaspoon TABASCO® brand Pepper Sauce

½ teaspoon ground coriander

1 pound boneless, skinless chicken breasts, cut into 1-inch pieces

Wooden skewers

Combine all ingredients except chicken and skewers in medium bowl. Add chicken; toss to coat. Cover and refrigerate 6 to 8 hours or overnight.

Preheat broiler or grill. Thread marinated chicken on skewers. Broil or grill 6 to 8 minutes, turning frequently. (Do not overcook.) Serve warm on skewers.

Makes 30 to 35 pieces

Helpful Hint

For best results, soak wooden skewers in water for about 30 minutes before using to make them more pliable and to prevent them from burning.

Thai Chicken Skewers

Greek-Style Sausage Roll

Prep Time: 30 minutes   **Cook Time:** 30 minutes

1 pound bulk sausage

¼ cup finely chopped onion

1 (10-ounce) package frozen chopped spinach, thawed and drained

¼ pound feta cheese, crumbled

¼ cup finely chopped parsley

⅛ teaspoon white pepper

1 egg, beaten

10 sheets frozen phyllo dough (17×13-inch rectangles), thawed

½ cup butter or margarine, melted

In large skillet, cook sausage and onion over medium-high heat until sausage is done and onion is tender, stirring occasionally. Drain. Stir in spinach, feta cheese, parsley, white pepper and egg. Set aside.

Preheat oven to 350°F. Unfold phyllo dough. Spread 1 sheet flat; top with another sheet of phyllo. Gently brush with some of melted butter. Top with remaining sheets of phyllo, brushing each with butter. Reserve 1 tablespoon butter for top of pastry.

Spread sausage-spinach mixture lengthwise over bottom third of layered phyllo dough to within 2 inches of ends. Fold ends over. Carefully roll up phyllo. Place roll, seam-side down, on lightly greased baking sheet; brush with reserved 1 tablespoon butter. Bake 30 to 35 minutes or until golden. To serve, cut into slices.

Makes 16 appetizer servings

Favorite recipe from **National Pork Board**

Roasted Sweet Pepper Tapas

2 red bell peppers (8 ounces each)

1 clove garlic, minced

1 teaspoon chopped fresh oregano leaves *or* ½ teaspoon dried oregano leaves, crushed

2 tablespoons olive oil

Garlic bread (optional)

Fresh oregano sprig for garnish

1. Cover broiler pan with foil. Set broiler pan about 4 inches from heat source. Preheat broiler. Place peppers on foil. Broil 15 to 20 minutes until blackened on all sides, turning peppers every 5 minutes with tongs.

2. To steam peppers and loosen skin, place blackened peppers in paper bag. Close bag; set aside to cool about 15 to 20 minutes.

3. To peel peppers, cut around core, twist and remove. Cut peppers in half; place pepper halves on cutting board. Peel off skin with paring knife; rinse under cold water to remove seeds.

4. Lay halves flat and slice lengthwise into ¼-inch strips with chef's knife.

5. Transfer pepper strips to glass jar. Add garlic, oregano and oil. Close lid; shake to blend. Marinate at least 1 hour. Serve on plates with garlic bread or refrigerate in jar up to 1 week. Garnish, if desired.

Makes 6 appetizer servings

Tip: Use this roasting technique for all types of sweet and hot peppers. Broiling time will vary depending on size of pepper. When handling hot peppers, such as Anaheim, jalapeño, poblano or serrano, wear plastic disposable gloves and use caution to prevent irritation of skin or eyes. Green bell peppers do not work as well since their skins are thinner.

Tex-Mex Polenta Shapes

2½ cups water

¾ cup yellow cornmeal

½ teaspoon salt

1¼ cups (5 ounces) shredded Mexican blend cheese, divided

⅓ cup finely diced red bell pepper

¼ cup chopped green onions

1 small jalapeño pepper, seeded and minced

Combine water, cornmeal and salt in large microwavable bowl. Cover and microwave at HIGH 4 minutes, stirring halfway through cooking time. Stir in ½ cup cheese, bell pepper, green onions and jalapeño pepper; cover and microwave at HIGH 1 minute. (Polenta will be thick.) Cover and let stand 2 minutes.

Grease 9-inch square baking dish or casserole. Spread cornmeal mixture into prepared dish. Cover and refrigerate 2 hours or until firm.

Preheat oven to 450°F. Spray baking sheet with nonstick cooking spray. Turn polenta out of baking dish onto cutting board; cut into circles, squares, triangles or other desired shapes with cookie cutters or sharp knife. Place polenta shapes on prepared baking sheet.

Bake about 7 minutes or until bottoms of polenta shapes are golden brown. Turn shapes over and bake 5 minutes more. Sprinkle shapes with remaining cheese; bake about 5 minutes or until cheese is lightly browned and bubbly. *Makes 1 to 2 dozen appetizers*

Tex-Mex Polenta Shapes

Barbecued Swedish Meatballs

MEATBALLS

1½ pounds lean ground beef

1 cup finely chopped onions

½ cup fresh breadcrumbs

½ cup HOLLAND HOUSE®
White Cooking Wine

1 egg, beaten

½ teaspoon allspice

½ teaspoon nutmeg

SAUCE

1 jar (10 ounces) currant jelly

½ cup chili sauce

¼ cup HOLLAND HOUSE®
White Cooking Wine

1 tablespoon cornstarch

Heat oven to 350°F. In medium bowl, combine all meatball ingredients, mix well. Shape into 1-inch balls. Place meatballs in 15×10×1-inch baking pan. Bake 20 minutes or until brown.

In medium saucepan, combine all sauce ingredients; mix well. Cook over medium heat until mixture boils and thickens, stirring occasionally. Add meatballs. To serve, place meatballs and sauce in fondue pot or chafing dish. Serve with cocktail picks.

Makes 6 to 8 servings

Helpful Hint

When shaping a ground beef mixture into meatballs, don't compact them too much or the meatballs will be tough. To prevent the mixture from sticking to your hands, dampen your hands before shaping the meatballs.

Barbecued Swedish Meatballs

Spiced Sesame Wonton Crisps

20 (3-inch square) wonton wrappers, cut in half

1 tablespoon water

2 teaspoons olive oil

½ teaspoon paprika

½ teaspoon ground cumin or chili powder

¼ teaspoon dry mustard

1 tablespoon sesame seeds

1. Preheat oven to 375°F. Coat 2 large nonstick baking sheets with nonstick cooking spray.

2. Cut each halved wonton wrapper into 2 strips; place in single layer on prepared baking sheets.

3. Combine water, oil, paprika, cumin and mustard in small bowl; mix well. Brush oil mixture evenly onto wonton strips; sprinkle evenly with sesame seeds.

4. Bake 6 to 8 minutes or until lightly browned. Remove to wire rack; cool completely. Transfer to serving plate.

Makes 8 servings

Stir-Fried Shrimp Appetizers

¼ cup KIKKOMAN® Soy Sauce

¼ cup dry white wine

¼ cup chopped green onions

1 clove garlic, pressed

1 teaspoon ground ginger

1 pound medium-size raw shrimp, peeled and deveined

3 tablespoons vegetable oil

Combine soy sauce, wine, green onions, garlic and ginger; stir in shrimp and let stand 15 minutes. Heat oil in hot wok or large skillet over medium-high heat. Drain shrimp and add to pan. Discard marinade. Stir-fry 1 to 2 minutes, or until shrimp are pink. Serve immediately.

Makes 8 servings

Spiced Sesame Wonton Crisps

Spanish Potato Omelet

¼ **cup olive oil**

¼ **cup vegetable oil**

1 **pound unpeeled red or white potatoes, cut into ⅛-inch slices**

½ **teaspoon salt, divided**

1 **small onion, cut in half lengthwise, thinly sliced crosswise**

¼ **cup chopped green bell pepper**

¼ **cup chopped red bell pepper**

3 **eggs**

Heat oils in large skillet over medium-high heat. Add potatoes to hot oil. Turn with spatula several times to coat all slices with oil. Sprinkle with ¼ teaspoon of the salt. Cook 6 to 9 minutes or until potatoes become translucent, turning occasionally. Add onion and peppers. Reduce heat to medium. Cook 10 minutes or until potatoes are tender, turning occasionally. Drain mixture in colander placed in large bowl; reserve oil. Let potato mixture stand until cool. Beat eggs with remaining ¼ teaspoon salt in large bowl. Gently stir in potato mixture; lightly press into bowl until mixture is covered with eggs. Let stand 15 minutes.

Heat 2 teaspoons reserved oil in 6-inch nonstick skillet over medium-high heat. Spread potato mixture in pan to form solid layer. Cook until egg on bottom and side of pan has set but top still looks moist. Cover pan with plate. Flip omelet onto plate, then slide omelet back into pan. Continue to cook until bottom is lightly browned. Slide omelet onto serving plate. Let stand 30 minutes before serving. Serve in wedges. *Makes 8 servings*

Asian Beef Bites

½ cup A.1.® THICK & HEARTY Steak Sauce

2 tablespoons sherry cooking wine

1 tablespoon PLANTERS® Peanut Oil

1 tablespoon Oriental sesame oil

1 tablespoon sesame seed, toasted

1 clove garlic, minced

1 teaspoon minced fresh ginger

1 (1-pound) beef top round steak, cut into ¾-inch cubes

18 snow peas, halved crosswise

Soak 18 (6-inch) wooden skewers in water at least 30 minutes.

In small bowl, combine steak sauce, sherry, peanut and sesame oils, sesame seed, garlic and ginger; set aside.

Thread steak and snow peas onto skewers, beginning and ending with 1 snow pea half; place in nonmetal dish. Pour reserved steak sauce mixture over skewers, turning to coat completely. Cover; refrigerate 1 hour, turning occasionally.

Remove skewers from marinade; reserve marinade. Grill skewers over medium heat or broil 6 inches from heat source 4 to 6 minutes or until steak is desired doneness, turning and basting once with marinade. (Discard any remaining marinade.) Serve immediately.

Makes 18 appetizers

Helpful Hint

If you don't have a ginger grater, a garlic press works just as well for mincing ginger. Place a small, peeled chunk of fresh ginger in the press and squeeze.

Mediterranean Pita Pizzas

1 cup rinsed and drained canned cannellini beans

2 teaspoons lemon juice

2 medium cloves garlic, minced

2 (8-inch) pita breads

1 teaspoon olive oil

½ cup thinly sliced radicchio or escarole lettuce (optional)

½ cup chopped seeded tomato

½ cup finely chopped red onion

¼ cup (1 ounce) crumbled feta cheese

2 tablespoons thinly sliced pitted black olives

1. Preheat oven to 450°F.

2. Place beans in small bowl; mash lightly with fork. Stir in lemon juice and garlic.

3. Arrange pitas on baking sheet; brush tops with oil. Bake 6 minutes.

4. Spread bean mixture evenly onto pita rounds to within ½ inch of edges. Arrange remaining ingredients evenly on pitas. Bake 5 minutes or until topping is thoroughly heated and crust is crisp. Cut into quarters. Serve hot. *Makes 8 servings*

Helpful Hint

Cannellini beans are cultivated large white beans used extensively in Italian cooking. Great Northern beans may be substituted.

Mediterranean Pita Pizzas

Awesome Antipasto

1 jar (16 ounces) mild cherry peppers, drained

1 jar (9 ounces) artichoke hearts, drained

½ pound asparagus spears, cooked

½ cup pitted black olives

1 red onion, cut into wedges

1 green bell pepper, sliced into rings

1 red bell pepper, sliced into rings

1 bottle (8 ounces) Italian salad dressing

1 cup shredded Parmesan cheese, divided

1 package (6 ounces) HILLSHIRE FARM® Hard Salami

Layer cherry peppers, artichoke hearts, asparagus, olives, onion and bell peppers in 13×9-inch glass baking dish.

Pour dressing and ⅓ cup cheese over vegetables. Cover; refrigerate 1 to 2 hours.

Drain vegetables, reserving marinade. Arrange vegetables and Hard Salami in rows on serving platter. Drizzle with reserved marinade. Top with remaining ⅔ cup cheese. *Makes 6 servings*

Helpful Hint

Antipasto is an Italian term that literally means "before the pasta," but generally refers to any hot or cold appetizers. Antipasto platters often include a selection of meats, cheeses, olives and marinated vegetables.

Bruschetta

Prep Time: 15 minutes   **Cook Time:** 30 minutes

1 can (14½ ounces) DEL MONTE® Diced Tomatoes, drained

2 tablespoons chopped fresh basil *or* ½ teaspoon dried basil

1 small clove garlic, finely minced

½ French bread baguette, cut into ⅜-inch-thick slices

2 tablespoons olive oil

1. Combine tomatoes, basil and garlic in 1-quart bowl; cover and refrigerate at least ½ hour.

2. Preheat broiler. Place bread slices on baking sheet; lightly brush both sides of bread with oil. Broil until lightly toasted, turning to toast both sides. Cool on wire rack.

3. Bring tomato mixture to room temperature. Spoon tomato mixture over bread and serve immediately. Sprinkle with additional fresh basil leaves, if desired.

Makes 8 appetizer servings

Note: For a fat-free version, omit olive oil. For a lower-fat variation, spray the bread with olive oil cooking spray.

Miniature Teriyaki Pork Kabobs

1 pound boneless pork, cut into 4×1×½-inch strips

1 small green bell pepper, cut into 1×¼×¼-inch strips

1 can (11 ounces) mandarin oranges, drained

¼ cup teriyaki sauce

1 tablespoon honey

1 tablespoon vinegar

⅛ teaspoon garlic powder

Soak 24 (8-inch) bamboo skewers in water 10 minutes. Thread 1 pepper strip, then pork strips accordion-style with mandarin oranges on skewers. Place 1 pepper strip on end of each skewer. Arrange skewers on broiler pan.

For sauce, combine teriyaki sauce, honey, vinegar and garlic powder in small bowl; mix well. Brush sauce over kabobs. Broil, 6 inches from heat, about 15 minutes or until pork is done, turning and basting with sauce occasionally.   *Makes about 24 appetizers*

Favorite recipe from **National Pork Board**

Apricot-Chicken Pot Stickers

2 cups plus 1 tablespoon water, divided

2 small boneless skinless chicken breasts (about 8 ounces)

2 cups chopped finely shredded cabbage

½ cup all-fruit apricot preserves

2 green onions with tops, finely chopped

2 teaspoons soy sauce

½ teaspoon grated fresh ginger

⅛ teaspoon black pepper

30 (3-inch) wonton wrappers

Prepared sweet & sour sauce (optional)

1. Bring 2 cups water to boil in medium saucepan. Add chicken. Reduce heat to low; simmer, covered, 10 minutes or until chicken is no longer pink in center. Remove from saucepan; drain.

2. Add cabbage and remaining 1 tablespoon water to saucepan. Cook over high heat 1 to 2 minutes or until water evaporates, stirring occasionally. Remove from heat; cool slightly.

3. Finely chop chicken. Add to saucepan along with preserves, green onions, soy sauce, ginger and pepper; mix well.

4. To assemble pot stickers, remove 3 wonton wrappers at a time from package. Spoon slightly rounded tablespoonful of chicken mixture onto center of each wrapper; brush edges with water. Bring 4 corners together; press to seal. Repeat with remaining wrappers and filling.

5. Spray steamer with nonstick cooking spray. Assemble steamer so that water is ½ inch below steamer basket. Fill steamer basket with pot stickers, leaving enough space between them to prevent sticking. Cover; steam 5 minutes. Transfer pot stickers to serving plate. Serve with prepared sweet & sour sauce, if desired.

Makes 10 servings (3 pot stickers each)

Apricot-Chicken Pot Stickers

Spanish-Style Garlic Shrimp

4 tablespoons I CAN'T BELIEVE IT'S NOT BUTTER!® Spread, divided

1 pound uncooked medium shrimp, peeled and deveined

½ teaspoon salt

2 cloves garlic, finely chopped

½ to 1 jalapeño pepper, seeded and finely chopped

¼ cup chopped fresh cilantro or parsley

1 tablespoon fresh lime juice

In 12-inch nonstick skillet, melt 1 tablespoon I Can't Believe It's Not Butter! Spread over high heat and cook shrimp with salt 2 minutes or until shrimp are almost pink, turning once. Remove shrimp and set aside.

In same skillet, melt remaining 3 tablespoons I Can't Believe It's Not Butter! Spread over medium-low heat and cook garlic and jalapeño pepper, stirring occasionally, 1 minute. Return shrimp to skillet. Stir in cilantro and lime juice and heat 30 seconds or until shrimp turn pink. Serve, if desired, with crusty Italian bread.

Makes 6 servings

Drums of Heaven

1 tablespoon KIKKOMAN® Soy Sauce

1 tablespoon dry sherry

18 chicken wing drumettes

⅓ cup KIKKOMAN® Teriyaki Baste & Glaze

1 large clove garlic, minced

2 teaspoons sesame seed, toasted

Preheat oven to 425°F. Combine soy sauce and sherry in large bowl; add drumettes. Toss until well coated. Arrange drumettes, in single layer, on large rack in shallow foil-lined baking pan. Bake 30 minutes. Meanwhile, combine teriyaki baste & glaze and garlic in small bowl; brush tops of drumettes with half of glaze. Turn pieces over; brush with remaining glaze. Bake 15 minutes longer or until chicken is no longer pink near bone; sprinkle with sesame seed.

Makes 6 servings

Spanish-Style Garlic Shrimp

Caribbean Chutney Kabobs

20 (4-inch) bamboo skewers

½ medium pineapple

1 medium red bell pepper, cut into 1-inch pieces

¾ pound boneless skinless chicken breasts, cut into 1-inch pieces

½ cup bottled mango chutney

2 tablespoons orange juice or pineapple juice

1 teaspoon vanilla

¼ teaspoon ground nutmeg

1. To prevent burning, soak skewers in water at least 20 minutes before assembling kabobs.

2. Peel and core pineapple. Cut pineapple into 1-inch chunks. Alternately thread bell pepper, pineapple and chicken onto skewers. Place in shallow baking dish.

3. Combine chutney, orange juice, vanilla and nutmeg in small bowl; mix well. Pour over kabobs; cover. Refrigerate up to 4 hours.

4. Preheat broiler. Spray broiler pan with nonstick cooking spray; place kabobs on prepared broiler pan. Broil, 6 to 8 inches from heat, 4 to 5 minutes on each side or until chicken is no longer pink in center. Transfer to serving plates. *Makes 10 servings*

Helpful Hint

Chutney is a spicy fruit-based relish served as a refreshing accompaniment to Indian curries. There are many variations—some raw, others cooked. The most well-known commercial chutney, Major Grey's, is made with mangoes cooked with raisins, tamarind, vinegar, sugar, ginger and spices. Commercial products in glass jars keep indefinitely in the refrigerator.

Caribbean Chutney Kabobs

Bavarian Crostini

¼ cup I CAN'T BELIEVE IT'S
NOT BUTTER!® Spread

1 large Spanish onion, thinly
sliced

½ teaspoon caraway seeds,
coarsely crushed
(optional)

½ teaspoon salt

24 round slices (¼ inch thick)
French or Italian bread

¼ pound thinly sliced
Jarlsberg or Swiss
cheese, quartered

Preheat oven to 375°F.

In 12-inch skillet, melt I Can't Believe It's Not Butter! Spread over
medium-high heat and cook onion, caraway seeds and salt, stirring
occasionally, 14 minutes or until onion is golden.

Meanwhile, on baking sheet, arrange bread slices. Bake 10 minutes
or until edges are golden.

Evenly top each bread slice with onion mixture, then cheese slices.
Bake 2 minutes or until cheese is melted. Serve hot.

Makes 24 crostini

Spicy Pork Strips

1 pound boneless pork
chops, ½ inch thick

⅓ cup KIKKOMAN® Soy Sauce

¼ cup minced green onions
and tops

1 tablespoon sugar

1 tablespoon sesame seed,
toasted

3 tablespoons water

1½ teaspoons minced fresh
ginger root

1 teaspoon hot pepper sauce

1 clove garlic, minced

Slice pork into ¼-inch-thick strips, about 4 inches long. Thread
onto bamboo or metal skewers, keeping meat as flat as possible.
Arrange pork skewers in large shallow pan. Blend soy sauce, green
onions, sugar, sesame seed, water, ginger, pepper sauce and garlic,
stirring until sugar dissolves. Pour mixture evenly over pork skewers;
turn over to coat all sides. Let stand 30 minutes, turning pork
skewers over occasionally. Reserving marinade, remove pork skewers
and place on rack of broiler pan; brush with reserved marinade.
Broil 3 minutes or until pork is tender, turning once and basting
with additional marinade. *Makes 6 to 8 appetizer servings*

Greek Grilled Pizza Wedges

⅓ cup prepared pizza sauce

¼ cup A.1.® Steak Sauce

4 (6-inch) whole wheat pita breads

2 tablespoons olive oil

4 ounces deli sliced roast beef, coarsely chopped

½ cup chopped tomato

⅓ cup sliced pitted ripe olives

½ cup crumbled feta cheese* (2 ounces)

*¾ cup shredded mozzarella cheese may be substituted.

Blend pizza sauce and steak sauce; set aside. Brush both sides of pita bread with oil. Spread sauce mixture on one side of each pita; top with roast beef, tomato, olives and feta cheese.

Grill prepared pita, topping side up, over medium heat for 4 to 5 minutes or until topping is hot and pita is crisp. Cut each pita into 4 wedges to serve.   *Makes 8 appetizer servings*

Crunchy Mexican Turkey Tidbits

1 pound ground turkey

1 egg, beaten

2 garlic cloves, minced

¼ cup each finely chopped onion and dry bread crumbs

1 teaspoon chili powder

½ teaspoon cumin

4 ounces tortilla chips, finely crushed

Nonstick cooking spray

¾ cup nonfat sour cream

½ cup salsa

1. In medium bowl combine turkey, egg, garlic, onion, bread crumbs, chili powder and cumin; shape into approximately 36 (¾-inch) balls.

2. Place crushed chips on plate. Roll each meatball in chips, coating thoroughly. On 15×10×1-inch baking pan lightly coated with nonstick cooking spray, arrange meatballs. Bake at 350°F 20 minutes or until meat is no longer pink in center.

3. In small bowl combine sour cream and salsa. Use as dip for meatballs.   *Makes 36 meatballs*

*Favorite recipe from **National Turkey Federation***

Sopes

4 cups masa harina flour
(Mexican corn masa mix)

½ cup vegetable shortening
or lard

2½ cups warm water

1 can (7 ounces) ORTEGA®
Diced Green Chiles

2 tablespoons vegetable oil,
divided

Toppings: warmed ORTEGA®
Refried Beans, shredded
mild Cheddar or
shredded Monterey Jack
cheese, ORTEGA® SALSA
PRIMA™ Thick & Chunky,
sour cream, ORTEGA®
Pickled Jalapeños Slices

PLACE flour in large bowl; cut in vegetable shortening with pastry blender or two knives until mixture resembles coarse crumbs. Gradually add water, kneading until smooth. Add chiles; mix well. Form dough into 35 small balls. Pat each ball into 3-inch patty; place on waxed paper.

HEAT 1 teaspoon oil in large skillet over medium-high heat for 1 to 2 minutes. Cook patties for 3 minutes on each side or until golden brown, adding additional oil as needed.

TOP with beans, cheese, salsa, dollop of sour cream and jalapeños.

Makes about 35 appetizer servings

Helpful Hint

Masa is the traditional dough used to make corn tortillas. Dried corn kernels are cooked, soaked overnight and then ground into masa. Masa harina is flour made from dried masa; it is available at some supermarkets and at neighborhood Latin markets.

Sopes

Vegetable Omelets

Korean Dipping Sauce
  (recipe follows)

2 tablespoons plus
    1 teaspoon vegetable oil,
    divided

1 large carrot, peeled and
    julienned

8 ounces ground pork

1 clove garlic, minced

8 eggs

½ teaspoon salt

¼ teaspoon black pepper

1 cup bean sprouts

½ cup chives, cut into
    1½-inch lengths

1. Prepare Korean Dipping Sauce; set aside.

2. Heat 1 tablespoon oil in wok or skillet over medium-high heat. Add carrot; stir-fry 2 minutes. Remove from wok. Add ground pork and garlic to wok. Stir-fry about 2 minutes or until pork is well browned. Set aside to cool.

3. Combine eggs, salt and pepper in medium bowl; beat with wire whisk or fork until frothy. Stir in bean sprouts, chives, carrot and pork mixture; mix well.

4. Spray 4 (8½-ounce) pineapple cans with tops and bottoms removed with nonstick cooking spray.

5. Heat 2 teaspoons oil to 300°F in nonstick electric skillet or large nonstick skillet over medium-high heat. Set cans in skillet; pour ½ cup egg mixture into each can. Lower heat to 250°F (medium-low); cover and cook about 3 minutes or until eggs are set.

6. Remove cans; turn omelets with spatula and cook 1 to 2 minutes more. Repeat with remaining oil and egg mixture.

7. Cut omelets into quarters; serve with Korean Dipping Sauce.

Makes 4 servings

Korean Dipping Sauce: Combine ¼ cup rice wine vinegar, 2 tablespoons soy sauce and 4 teaspoons sugar in small bowl; stir until sugar is dissolved.

Vegetable Omelets

Mustard-Glazed Shrimp

Prep Time: 20 minutes   **Broil Time:** 10 minutes

MAZOLA NO STICK®
Cooking Spray

1 tablespoon dry mustard

2 tablespoons hot water

¼ cup KARO® Light or Dark
Corn Syrup

¼ cup prepared duck or plum
sauce

2 tablespoons rice wine or
sake

1 tablespoon soy sauce

1 tablespoon dark Oriental
sesame oil

1 pound large shrimp, shelled
and deveined, or sea
scallops

¾ pound sliced bacon, cut
crosswise in half

Bamboo skewers, soaked in
cold water 20 minutes

1. Line broiler pan rack with foil; spray with cooking spray.

2. In small bowl stir mustard and water until smooth. Stir in corn syrup, duck sauce, rice wine, soy sauce and sesame oil.

3. In large bowl toss shrimp with about ¼ cup of the mustard glaze. Wrap half slice bacon around each shrimp and thread about 1 inch apart onto skewers.

4. Broil 6 inches from heat, 8 to 10 minutes or until shrimp are tender, turning and brushing occasionally with remaining mustard glaze.

Makes 6 to 8 appetizer servings

Seoul Rolled Beef with Vegetables

2 carrots, cut into thin strips

2 parsnips, cut into thin strips

8 small green beans, halved lengthwise

4 thin slices beef top round steak (7 to 8 ounces each), each sliced crosswise into 2 pieces

4 tablespoons vegetable oil, divided

1 can (about 14 ounces) beef broth, divided

1 piece fresh ginger (about 1½ inches long), peeled and cut into 6 (¼-inch-thick) slices

¼ teaspoon ground red pepper

1 tablespoon rice wine or dry sherry

1 tablespoon soy sauce

1 teaspoon sugar

1 teaspoon cornstarch

1 teaspoon sesame oil

1 small ripe tomato, cut into wedges

Lettuce leaves

Kimchee* (optional)

*Kimchee is a spicy-hot, pungent condiment made of fermented vegetables (usually cabbage or turnips) served at almost every Korean meal. It is available in Asian markets.

1. Place ⅛ of carrots, ⅛ of parsnips and 2 green bean halves on each piece of beef along one short end. Starting with short end, roll up beef, jelly-roll fashion, to enclose vegetables; secure with short bamboo or metal skewers.

2. Heat wok over high heat 1 minute or until hot. Drizzle 2 tablespoons vegetable oil into wok.

3. Add 4 beef rolls. Cook rolls 2½ to 3 minutes or until browned on all sides, turning occasionally. Transfer to bowl. Reheat wok and repeat with remaining 2 tablespoons vegetable oil and 4 beef rolls.

4. Return all rolls to wok. Add 1 cup broth, ginger and red pepper. Cover and bring to a boil. Reduce heat to low; simmer rolls 1 hour or until beef is fork-tender, turning to cook evenly. Add more broth if it evaporates. Transfer cooked rolls to cutting board.

5. Pour cooking liquid from wok into glass measuring cup. Discard ginger. Add enough broth or water to make ⅔ cup liquid; return to wok and bring to a boil. Meanwhile, combine rice wine, soy sauce, sugar, cornstarch and sesame oil in small bowl; mix well and add to wok. Cook and stir until liquid boils and thickens. Pour sauce into small bowl.

6. Remove skewers from beef rolls. Cut rolls in half diagonally. Arrange on lettuce-lined platter. Garnish with tomato wedges. Serve with kimchee, if desired. *Makes 4 servings*

Jerk Wings with Ranch Dipping Sauce

½ cup mayonnaise

½ cup plain yogurt or sour cream

1½ teaspoons salt, divided

1¼ teaspoons garlic powder, divided

½ teaspoon black pepper, divided

¼ teaspoon onion powder

2 tablespoons orange juice

1 teaspoon sugar

1 teaspoon dried thyme leaves

1 teaspoon paprika

¼ teaspoon ground nutmeg

¼ teaspoon ground red pepper

2½ pounds chicken wings (about 10 wings)

For Ranch Dipping Sauce, combine mayonnaise, yogurt, ½ teaspoon salt, ¼ teaspoon garlic powder, ¼ teaspoon black pepper and onion powder in small bowl.

Preheat oven to 450°F.

Combine orange juice, sugar, thyme, paprika, nutmeg, red pepper, remaining 1 teaspoon salt, 1 teaspoon garlic powder and ¼ teaspoon black pepper in small bowl.

Cut tips from wings; discard. Place wings in large bowl. Drizzle with orange juice mixture; toss to coat.

Transfer chicken to greased broiler pan. Bake 25 to 30 minutes or until juices run clear and skin is crisp. Serve with Ranch Dipping Sauce.

Makes 6 to 7 servings

Serving Suggestion: Serve with celery sticks.

Jerk Wings with Ranch Dipping Sauce

Tuscan White Bean Crostini

2 cans (15 ounces each) white beans (such as Great Northern or cannellini), rinsed and drained

½ large red bell pepper, finely chopped *or* ⅓ cup finely chopped roasted red bell pepper

⅓ cup finely chopped onion

⅓ cup red wine vinegar

3 tablespoons chopped fresh parsley

1 tablespoon olive oil

2 cloves garlic, minced

½ teaspoon dried oregano leaves

¼ teaspoon black pepper

18 French bread slices, about ¼ inch thick

1. Combine beans, bell pepper and onion in large bowl.

2. Whisk together vinegar, parsley, oil, garlic, oregano and black pepper in small bowl. Pour over bean mixture; toss to coat. Cover; refrigerate 2 hours or overnight.

3. Arrange bread slices in single layer on large nonstick baking sheet or broiler pan. Broil, 6 to 8 inches from heat, 30 to 45 seconds or until bread slices are lightly toasted. Remove; cool completely.

4. Top each toasted bread slice with about 3 tablespoons of bean mixture.

Makes 6 servings

Helpful Hint

There's no need to peel the garlic cloves before running them through a garlic press. After squeezing the clove in the press, the skin will remain behind; discard the skin before pressing the next clove through.

Tuscan White Bean Crostini

Italian-Style Stuffed Mushrooms

2 pounds large mushrooms (about 2 inches each)

½ cup (1 stick) I CAN'T BELIEVE IT'S NOT BUTTER!® Spread

⅓ cup chopped onion

1 tablespoon chopped garlic

1 cup Italian seasoned dry bread crumbs

⅔ cup shredded mozzarella cheese (about 2½ ounces)

¼ cup grated Parmesan cheese

2 tablespoons chopped fresh parsley

1 tablespoon red wine vinegar

⅛ teaspoon ground black pepper

¼ teaspoon salt

Preheat oven to 400°F.

Remove and chop mushroom stems.

In 12-inch skillet, melt I Can't Believe It's Not Butter! Spread over medium-high heat and cook mushroom stems and onion, stirring occasionally, 5 minutes or until tender.

Add garlic and cook 30 seconds. In medium bowl, pour mushroom mixture over bread crumbs. Stir in cheeses, parsley, vinegar and pepper.

Sprinkle mushroom caps with salt. On baking sheet, arrange mushroom caps; evenly spoon mushroom mixture into mushroom caps.

Bake 25 minutes or until mushrooms are tender and golden.

Makes about 20 mushrooms

Chili-Cheese Quesadillas with Salsa Cruda

2 tablespoons part-skim
  ricotta cheese

6 (6-inch) corn tortillas

½ cup (2 ounces) shredded
  reduced fat Monterey
  Jack cheese

2 tablespoons diced mild
  green chilies

  Nonstick cooking spray

  Salsa Cruda (recipe follows)

1. To make 1 quesadilla, spread 2 teaspoons ricotta over tortilla. Sprinkle with heaping tablespoonful Monterey Jack cheese and 2 teaspoons diced chilies. Top with 1 tortilla. Repeat to make 2 more quesadillas.

2. Spray small nonstick skillet with cooking spray. Heat over medium-high heat. Add 1 quesadilla; cook 2 minutes or until bottom is golden. Turn quesadilla over; cook 2 minutes. Remove from heat. Cut into 4 wedges. Repeat with remaining quesadillas. Serve warm with Salsa Cruda. *Makes 4 servings*

Salsa Cruda

  1 cup chopped tomato

  2 tablespoons minced onion

  2 tablespoons minced fresh cilantro (optional)

  2 tablespoons lime juice

  ½ jalapeño pepper,* seeded, minced

  1 clove garlic, minced

Jalapeño peppers can sting and irritate the skin; wear rubber gloves when handling peppers and do not touch eyes. Wash hands after handling peppers.

1. Combine tomato, onion, cilantro, lime juice, jalapeño and garlic in small bowl. Stir to combine. *Makes 4 servings*

French-Style Pizza Bites (Pissaladière)

2 tablespoons olive oil

1 medium onion, thinly sliced

1 medium red bell pepper, cut into strips

2 cloves garlic, minced

⅓ cup pitted black olives, each cut into thin wedges

1 can (10 ounces) refrigerated pizza crust dough

¾ cup (3 ounces) finely shredded Swiss or Gruyère cheese

1. Position oven rack to lowest position. Preheat oven to 425°F. Grease large baking sheet.

2. Heat oil until hot in medium skillet over medium heat. Add onion, pepper and garlic. Cook and stir 5 minutes or until vegetables are crisp-tender. Stir in olives; remove from heat.

3. Pat dough into 16×12-inch rectangle on prepared baking sheet.

4. Arrange vegetables over dough; sprinkle with cheese. Bake 10 minutes. Loosen crust from baking sheet; slide crust onto oven rack. Bake 3 to 5 minutes or until golden brown.

5. Slide baking sheet back under crust to remove crust from rack. Transfer to cutting board. Cut dough crosswise into eight 1¾-inch-wide strips. Cut dough diagonally into ten 2-inch-wide strips, making diamond pieces. Serve immediately.

Makes about 24 servings (2 diamonds per serving)

French-Style Pizza Bites (Pissaladière)

Special Occasions

Mini Chick-Pea Cakes

1 can (15 ounces) chick-peas (garbanzo beans), rinsed and drained

1 cup shredded carrots

⅓ cup seasoned dry bread crumbs

¼ cup creamy Italian salad dressing

1 egg

Preheat oven to 375°F. Spray baking sheet with nonstick cooking spray.

Mash chick-peas coarsely in medium bowl with hand potato masher. Stir in carrots, bread crumbs, salad dressing and egg; mix well.

Shape chick-pea mixture into small patties, using about 1 tablespooon mixture for each. Place on prepared baking sheet.

Bake 15 to 18 minutes, turning halfway through baking time, until chick-pea cakes are lightly browned on both sides. Serve warm with additional salad dressing for dipping, if desired.

Makes about 2 dozen

Mini Chick-Pea Cakes

Shrimp and Snow Pea Appetizers with Currant Mustard Sauce

6 ounces fresh snow peas
(about 36)

1½ pounds medium shrimp,
cooked and peeled

CURRANT MUSTARD SAUCE

¾ cup SMUCKER'S® Currant
Jelly

¼ cup Dijon mustard

Blanch snow peas in boiling salted water for 45 seconds. Immediately drain and run under cold water.

Wrap 1 blanched pea pod around each shrimp and secure with toothpick.

Combine jelly and mustard; beat with a fork or wire whisk until smooth. (Jelly will dissolve in about 5 minutes.) Serve sauce with appetizers.

Makes 36 appetizers

Eggplant Caviar

1 large eggplant, unpeeled

¼ cup chopped onion

2 tablespoons lemon juice

1 tablespoon olive *or*
vegetable oil

1 small clove garlic

½ teaspoon salt

½ teaspoon TABASCO® brand
Pepper Sauce

Sieved egg white (optional)

Lemon slices (optional)

Preheat oven to 350°F. Place eggplant in shallow baking dish. Bake 1 hour or until soft, turning once. Trim off ends; slice eggplant in half lengthwise. Place cut-side-down in colander and let drain 10 minutes. Scoop out pulp; reserve pulp and peel. Combine eggplant peel, onion, lemon juice, oil, garlic, salt and TABASCO® Sauce in blender or food processor. Cover and process until peel is finely chopped. Add eggplant pulp. Cover and process just until chopped. Place in serving dish. Garnish with egg white and lemon slices, if desired. Serve with toast points.

Makes 1½ cups

Shrimp and Snow Pea Appetizers with Currant Mustard Sauce

Rosemary-Roasted Vegetable Crostini

1 small eggplant (about ¾ pound)

1 medium zucchini

1 medium red onion

1 medium green bell pepper

2 Italian plum tomatoes, seeded

¼ cup dry white wine or orange juice

2 tablespoons tarragon white wine vinegar

4 medium cloves garlic, minced

1 tablespoon olive oil

1 tablespoon chopped fresh rosemary *or* 1 teaspoon dried rosemary, crushed

¼ teaspoon black pepper

1 loaf (1 pound) sourdough bread, 12 to 14 inches long

1 cup (4 ounces) shredded part-skim mozzarella cheese

1. Preheat oven to 400°F. Spray large nonstick baking sheets with nonstick cooking spray; set aside

2. Trim ends from eggplant and zucchini; discard. Cut all vegetables into ¼-inch pieces. Place vegetables in large bowl. Add wine, vinegar, garlic, oil and seasonings; toss to coat evenly. Transfer to nonstick 15×10×1-inch jelly-roll pan.

3. Bake 45 minutes or until lightly browned, stirring every 15 minutes.

4. Trim ends from bread; cut into ½-inch-thick slices. Arrange slices in single layer on prepared baking sheets. Bake 3 minutes on each side or until crisp and lightly browned on both sides.

5. Spoon vegetable mixture evenly onto toasted bread slices; sprinkle evenly with cheese. Continue baking 5 minutes or until mixture is heated through and cheese is melted. Transfer to serving plates; garnish, if desired.

Makes 12 servings

Rosemary-Roasted Vegetable Crostini

Southwestern Cheesecake

Prep Time: 20 minutes plus refrigerating   **Bake Time:** 30 minutes

1 cup finely crushed tortilla chips

3 tablespoons butter *or* margarine, melted

2 packages (8 ounces) PHILADELPHIA® Cream Cheese, softened

2 eggs

1 package (8 ounces) KRAFT® Shredded Colby/Monterey Jack Cheese

1 (4-ounce) can chopped green chilies, drained

1 cup BREAKSTONE'S® *or* KNUDSEN® Sour Cream

1 cup chopped yellow *or* orange bell pepper

½ cup green onion slices

⅓ cup chopped tomatoes

¼ cup sliced pitted ripe olives

MIX chips and butter in small bowl; press onto bottom of 9-inch springform pan. Bake at 325°F for 15 minutes.

BEAT cream cheese and eggs at medium speed with electric mixer until well blended. Mix in shredded cheese and chilies; pour over crust. Bake for 30 minutes.

SPREAD sour cream over cheesecake. Loosen cake from rim of pan; cool before removing rim of pan. Chill.

TOP with remaining ingredients just before serving.

Makes 16 to 20 appetizer servings

Note: To make an attractive design on top of this cheesecake, cut three diamonds out of paper. Place on top of cheesecake. Place green onion slices around diamonds. Remove cutouts; fill in with bell peppers. Add a strip of tomatoes down the center. Garnish with olives.

Helpful Hint

Prebaking a crumb crust helps to keep it crisp. Allow it to cool completely before filling.

Egg Rolls

Sweet and Sour Sauce
(recipe follows)

3 green onions, finely
chopped

3 cloves garlic, finely
chopped

½ teaspoon ground ginger

½ pound boneless skinless
chicken breasts, cooked
and finely chopped

2 cups bean sprouts, rinsed
and drained

½ cup shredded carrots

2 tablespoons reduced-
sodium soy sauce

¼ teaspoon black pepper

8 egg roll wrappers

2 teaspoons vegetable oil

1. Prepare Sweet and Sour Sauce.

2. Spray large nonstick skillet with cooking spray. Heat over
medium-high heat until hot. Add onions, garlic and ginger.
Cook and stir 1 minute. Add chicken, bean sprouts and carrots.
Cook and stir 2 minutes. Stir in soy sauce and pepper. Cook and
stir 1 minute. Remove skillet from heat. Let mixture stand
10 minutes or until cool enough to handle.

3. Brush edges of egg roll wrappers with water. Spoon filling evenly
down centers of wrappers. Fold ends over fillings; roll up jelly-roll
fashion.

4. Heat oil in another large nonstick skillet over medium heat until
hot. Add rolls. Cook 3 to 5 minutes or until golden brown,
turning occasionally. Serve hot with Sweet and Sour Sauce.

Makes 4 servings

Sweet and Sour Sauce: Bring 1 cup water, ½ cup white vinegar,
½ cup sugar and 4 teaspoons cornstarch to a boil in small saucepan
over high heat, stirring constantly. Boil 1 minute, stirring constantly.
Set aside to cool.

Spinach Cheese Bundles

1 container (6½ ounces) garlic- and herb-flavored spreadable cheese

½ cup chopped fresh spinach

¼ teaspoon pepper

1 package (17¼ ounces) frozen puff pastry, thawed

Sweet and sour or favorite dipping sauce (optional)

Preheat oven to 400°F. Combine spreadable cheese, spinach and pepper in small bowl; mix well.

Roll out one sheet puff pastry dough on floured surface into 12-inch square. Cut into 16 (3-inch) squares. Place about 1 teaspoon cheese mixture in center of each square. Brush edges of squares with water. Bring edges together up over filling and twist tightly to seal; fan out corners of puff pastry.

Place bundles 2 inches apart on baking sheet. Bake about 13 minutes or until golden brown. Repeat with remaining sheet of puff pastry and cheese mixture. Serve with dipping sauce, if desired. *Makes 32 bundles*

Pineapple-Champagne Punch

1 quart pineapple sherbet

1 quart unsweetened pineapple juice, chilled

1 bottle (750 ml) dry champagne, chilled

2 fresh or canned pineapple slices, each cut into 6 wedges

Mint sprigs

Process sherbet and pineapple juice in blender until smooth and frothy. Pour into punch bowl. Stir in champagne.

Float pineapple wedges in punch in groups of 3 or 4 to form flowers; garnish with mint sprigs. Serve immediately. *Makes 20 (4-ounce) servings*

Spinach Cheese Bundles

Honeyed Pork and Mango Kabobs

Prep Time: 30 minutes   **Marinate Time:** 1 hour   **Cook Time:** about 20 minutes

½ cup honey

¼ cup frozen apple juice concentrate, thawed

3 tablespoons *Frank's®
RedHot®* Cayenne Pepper Sauce

¼ teaspoon ground allspice

1 teaspoon grated lemon peel

1 pound pork tenderloin, cut into 1-inch cubes

1 large (12 ounces) ripe mango, peeled, pitted and cut into ¾-inch cubes, divided

½ cup frozen large baby onions, partially thawed

1. Combine honey, juice concentrate, *Frank's RedHot* and allspice in small saucepan. Bring to a boil over medium heat. Reduce heat to low; cook, stirring, 5 minutes. Stir in lemon peel. Remove from heat. Pour ¼ cup marinade into small bowl; reserve.

2. Place pork in large resealable plastic food storage bag. Pour remaining marinade over pork. Seal bag; refrigerate 1 hour. Prepare grill.

3. To prepare dipping sauce, place ¼ cup mango cubes in blender or food processor. Add reserved ¼ cup marinade. Cover; process until puréed. Transfer to serving bowl; set aside.

4. Alternately thread pork, remaining mango cubes and onions onto metal skewers. Place skewers on oiled grid. Grill,* over medium-low coals, 12 to 15 minutes or until pork is no longer pink. Serve kabobs with dipping sauce.   *Makes 6 servings (¾ cup sauce)*

Or, broil 6 inches from heat 10 to 12 minutes or until pork is no longer pink.

Note: You may substitute 1½ cups fresh or frozen peach cubes (2 to 3 peaches) for fresh mango.

Honeyed Pork and Mango Kabobs

Polenta Strips with Creamy Salsa Spread

1 package (8 ounces) cream cheese, softened

2 tablespoons chili sauce

2 tablespoons dairy sour cream

1 tablespoon diced green chiles

½ teaspoon LAWRY'S® Seasoned Pepper

3 cups water

1 teaspoon LAWRY'S® Seasoned Salt

¾ cup instant polenta, uncooked

¼ cup chopped fresh cilantro

¼ cup grated Parmesan cheese

½ cup vegetable oil

For Creamy Salsa Spread, in small bowl, combine cream cheese, chili sauce, sour cream, green chiles and Seasoned Pepper; mix well. Refrigerate at least one hour until chilled. In medium saucepan, combine water and Seasoned Salt. Bring to a boil over medium-high heat. Add polenta in a slow stream, stirring constantly. Reduce heat to low; simmer, uncovered, 20 minutes or until mixture pulls away from side of pan. Stir in cilantro. Pour mixture into lightly greased 8×4×3-inch loaf pan. Let cool at least 30 minutes to set. Remove from pan. Cut loaf into very thin slices; sprinkle both sides with cheese. Broil 3 inches from heat 5 minutes or until slightly golden brown. In large skillet, heat oil and fry slices until brown and crisp. Place on paper towels to drain. Serve with Creamy Salsa Spread.

Makes 3 dozen strips

Serving Suggestion: Great with grilled beef, pork or chicken entrees.

Hint: To prepare in advance, prepare recipe up to loaf stage, then refrigerate (up to 2 weeks) until ready to fry.

Roast Beef Crostini with Spicy Horseradish Sauce

1 baguette French bread

½ cup mayonnaise

4 tablespoons prepared horseradish, drained

1 teaspoon TABASCO® brand Pepper Sauce

8 ounces roast beef, cooked medium rare, thinly sliced*

Fresh ground pepper

*Deli sliced roast beef may be substituted.

Slice baguette into rounds ½ inch thick. Toast bread in toaster oven or broiler until light brown on both sides. Set aside.

Blend mayonnaise, horseradish and TABASCO® Sauce in small bowl. Spread generously on toast rounds. Top with roast beef slices; sprinkle with pepper.

Makes about 30 crostini

Cold Asparagus with Lemon-Mustard Dressing

12 fresh asparagus spears

2 tablespoons mayonnaise

1 tablespoon sweet brown mustard

1 tablespoon fresh lemon juice

1 teaspoon grated lemon peel, divided

1. Steam asparagus until crisp-tender and bright green; immediately drain and rinse under cold water. Cover and refrigerate until chilled.

2. Combine mayonnaise, mustard and lemon juice in small bowl; blend well. Stir in ½ teaspoon lemon peel; set aside.

3. Divide asparagus between 2 plates. Spoon 2 tablespoons dressing over top of each serving; sprinkle each with ¼ teaspoon lemon peel. Garnish with carrot strips, if desired.

Makes 2 appetizer servings

Oysters Romano

12 oysters, shucked and on the half shell

2 slices bacon, cut into 12 (1-inch) pieces

½ cup Italian-seasoned dry bread crumbs

2 tablespoons butter or margarine, melted

½ teaspoon garlic salt

6 tablespoons grated Romano, Parmesan or provolone cheese

Fresh chives for garnish

Preheat oven to 375°F. Place shells with oysters on baking sheet. Top each oyster with 1 piece bacon. Bake 10 minutes or until bacon is crisp. Meanwhile, combine bread crumbs, butter and garlic salt in small bowl. Spoon mixture over oysters; top with cheese. Bake 5 to 10 minutes or until cheese melts. Garnish with chives, if desired. Serve immediately.

Makes 4 appetizer servings

Stuffed Portobello Mushrooms

4 portobello mushrooms (4 ounces each)

¼ cup olive oil

2 cloves garlic, pressed

6 ounces crumbled goat cheese

2 ounces prosciutto or thinly sliced ham, chopped

¼ cup chopped fresh basil

Mixed salad greens

Remove stems and gently scrape gills from underside of mushrooms; discard stems and gills. Brush mushroom caps with combined oil and garlic. Combine cheese, prosciutto and basil in medium bowl. Grill mushrooms, top side up, on covered grill over medium KINGSFORD® Briquets 4 minutes. Turn mushrooms over; fill caps with cheese mixture, dividing equally. Cover and grill 3 to 4 minutes longer until cheese mixture is warm. Remove mushrooms from grill; cut into quarters. Serve on mixed greens.

Makes 4 servings

Oysters Romano

Honey-Nut Glazed Brie

8 ounces Brie cheese (wedge or round)

¼ cup I CAN'T BELIEVE IT'S NOT BUTTER!® Spread

1 cup coarsely chopped walnuts

¼ teaspoon ground cinnamon (optional)

⅛ teaspoon ground nutmeg (optional)

2 tablespoons honey

2 large green and/or red apples, cored and thinly sliced

Arrange cheese* on serving platter; set aside.

In 10-inch nonstick skillet, melt I Can't Believe It's Not Butter! Spread over medium-high heat and stir in walnuts until coated. Stir in cinnamon and nutmeg until blended. Stir in honey and cook, stirring constantly, 2 minutes or until mixture is bubbling. Immediately pour over cheese. Serve hot with apples.

Makes 8 servings

If desired, on microwave-safe plate, arrange cheese and top with cooked nut mixture. Microwave at HIGH (Full Power) 2 to 3 minutes or until cheese is warm. OR, in 1-quart shallow casserole, arrange cheese and top with cooked nut mixture. Bake at 350° for 10 minutes or until Brie just begins to melt. Serve as above.

Helpful Hint

Brie is a soft-ripened cheese. It should be stored tightly wrapped in the coldest part of the refrigerator for no more than two weeks. Any appearance of mold means the cheese should be thrown out (unlike firm, semifirm and semisoft cheeses, where spots of mold can be cut out and the cheese is still good).

Honey-Nut Glazed Brie

Coconut Chicken Tenders with Spicy Mango Salsa

1 firm ripe mango, peeled, seeded and chopped

½ cup chopped red bell pepper

3 tablespoons chopped green onion

2 tablespoons chopped fresh cilantro

1½ cups flaked coconut

1 egg

1 tablespoon vegetable oil

¼ teaspoon salt

Dash ground red pepper

¾ pound chicken tenders

For salsa, combine mango, bell pepper, onion and cilantro in small bowl.

Season to taste with salt and ground red pepper. Transfer half of salsa to food processor; process until finely chopped (almost puréed). Combine with remaining salsa.

Preheat oven to 400°F. Spread coconut on large baking sheet. Bake 5 to 6 minutes or until lightly browned, stirring every 2 minutes. Transfer coconut to food processor; process until finely chopped but not pasty.

Beat egg with oil, salt and red pepper in small bowl. Add chicken tenders; toss to coat. Roll tenders in coconut; arrange on foil-lined baking sheet. Bake 18 to 20 minutes or until no longer pink in center. Serve with Spicy Mango Salsa.   *Makes 5 to 6 servings*

Helpful Hint

Mangoes have thin, tough green skin that becomes yellow with tinges of red as they become ripe. Underripe mangoes can be placed in a paper bag to ripen at room temperature for several days. Store ripe mangoes in the refrigerator for up to five days.

Coconut Chicken Tenders with Spicy Mango Salsa

Marinated Antipasto Kabobs

½ (9-ounce) package spinach three-cheese tortellini or plain tortellini

1 package (9 ounces) frozen artichoke hearts, thawed

20 small fresh mushrooms, stems removed

1 large red bell pepper, cut into 20 equal-sized pieces

½ cup white balsamic or white wine vinegar

¼ cup (1 ounce) grated Parmesan cheese

¼ cup minced fresh basil

2 tablespoons Dijon mustard

1 tablespoon olive oil

½ teaspoon sugar

¼ teaspoon black pepper

20 cherry tomatoes

1. Cook tortellini according to package directions. Drain well. Cool slightly; cover and refrigerate until ready to assemble kabobs.

2. Cook artichokes according to package directions; drain. Immediately add artichokes to bowl of ice water to stop cooking process. Let stand 1 to 2 minutes; drain well. Place artichokes in large resealable plastic food storage bag. Add mushrooms and bell pepper.

3. Combine vinegar, cheese, basil, mustard, oil, sugar and black pepper in small bowl; mix well. Add to vegetable mixture in plastic bag; seal bag. Turn bag over several times to coat ingredients evenly. Refrigerate several hours or overnight, turning bag occasionally.

4. Remove vegetables from marinade, reserving marinade. Arrange vegetables on skewers alternately with tortellini and tomatoes; place on serving platter. Drizzle with reserved marinade, if desired. *Makes 20 kabobs*

Tip: Don't clean mushrooms until just before you're ready to use them (they will absorb water and become mushy). Wipe them with a damp paper towel or rinse them under cold running water and blot dry.

Roasted Red Pepper Pesto Cheesecake

Prep Time: 15 minutes plus refrigerating   **Bake Time:** 1 hour plus standing

1 cup butter-flavored cracker
  crumbs (about
  40 crackers)

¼ cup (½ stick) butter *or*
  margarine, melted

2 packages (8 ounces each)
  PHILADELPHIA® Cream
  Cheese, softened

1 cup ricotta cheese

3 eggs

½ cup KRAFT® 100% Grated
  Parmesan Cheese

½ cup DI GIORNO® Pesto

½ cup drained roasted red
  peppers, puréed

MIX crumbs and butter. Press onto bottom of 9-inch springform pan. Bake at 325°F for 10 minutes.

MIX cream cheese and ricotta cheese with electric mixer on medium speed until well blended. Add eggs, 1 at a time, mixing well after each addition. Blend in remaining ingredients. Pour over crust.

BAKE at 325°F for 55 minutes to 1 hour or until center is almost set. Run knife or metal spatula around rim of pan to loosen cake; cool before removing rim of pan. Refrigerate 4 hours or overnight. Let stand at room temperature 15 minutes before serving. Store leftover cheesecake in refrigerator.   *Makes 12 to 14 servings*

Mini Pizzas

CRUST

⅓ cup olive oil

1 tablespoon TABASCO®
     brand Pepper Sauce

2 large cloves garlic, crushed

1 teaspoon dried rosemary,
     crumbled

1 (16-ounce) package hot roll
     mix with yeast packet

1¼ cups hot water

GOAT CHEESE TOPPING

1 large tomato, diced

¼ cup crumbled goat cheese

2 tablespoons chopped fresh
     parsley

**ROASTED PEPPER AND OLIVE
TOPPING**

½ cup shredded mozzarella
     cheese

½ cup pitted green olives

⅓ cup roasted red pepper
     strips

ARTICHOKE TOPPING

½ cup chopped artichoke
     hearts

½ cup cherry tomatoes, sliced
     into wedges

⅓ cup sliced green onions

For crust, combine olive oil, TABASCO® Sauce, garlic and rosemary in small bowl. Combine hot roll mix, yeast packet, hot water and 2 tablespoons oil mixture in large bowl; stir until dough pulls away from side of bowl. Turn dough onto lightly floured surface; shape into ball. Knead until smooth, adding additional flour as necessary.

Preheat oven to 425°F. For toppings, combine ingredients in separate bowls. Cut dough into quarters; cut each quarter into 10 equal pieces. Roll each piece into a ball. Press each ball into 2-inch round on large cookie sheet; brush each round with remaining oil mixture. Arrange about 2 teaspoons topping on each dough round. Bake 12 minutes or until dough is lightly browned and puffed.

Makes 40 appetizers

Mini Pizzas

Savory Stuffed Mushrooms

Preparation Time: 20 minutes   **Cook Time:** 15 minutes   **Total Time:** 35 minutes

20 medium mushrooms

2 tablespoons finely chopped onion

2 tablespoons finely chopped red bell pepper

3 tablespoons FLEISCHMANN'S® Original Margarine

½ cup dry seasoned bread crumbs

½ teaspoon dried basil leaves

1. Remove stems from mushrooms; finely chop ¼ cup stems.

2. Cook and stir chopped stems, onion and pepper in margarine in skillet over medium heat until tender. Remove from heat; stir in crumbs and basil.

3. Spoon crumb mixture loosely into mushroom caps; place on baking sheet. Bake at 400°F for 15 minutes or until hot.

Makes 20 appetizers

Almond Chicken Cups

1 tablespoon vegetable oil

½ cup chopped red bell pepper

½ cup chopped onion

2 cups chopped cooked chicken

⅔ cup prepared sweet-sour sauce

½ cup chopped almonds

2 tablespoons soy sauce

6 (6- or 7-inch) flour tortillas

1. Preheat oven to 400°F. Heat oil in small skillet over medium heat until hot. Add bell pepper and onion. Cook and stir 3 minutes or until crisp-tender.

2. Combine vegetable mixture, chicken, sweet-sour sauce, almonds and soy sauce in medium bowl; mix until well blended.

3. Cut each tortilla in half. Place each half in 2¾-inch muffin cup. Fill each with about ¼ cup chicken mixture.

4. Bake 8 to 10 minutes or until tortilla edges are crisp and filling is hot. Remove muffin pan to cooling rack. Let stand 5 minutes before serving.

Makes 12 chicken cups

Colorado Potato Pancake Appetizers

1 pound (2 medium)
   Colorado potatoes,
   peeled and shredded

1 egg

2 tablespoons all-purpose
   flour

1 teaspoon salt

¼ teaspoon pepper

1½ cups shredded zucchini
   (2 small)

1 cup shredded carrots

Olive oil

½ cup low-fat sour cream or
   plain yogurt

2 tablespoons finely chopped
   basil plus 1 tablespoon
   chopped chives *or*
   1½ teaspoons chili
   powder or curry powder

Heat oven to 425°F. Wrap shredded potatoes in several layers of paper towels; squeeze to wring out much of liquid. In large bowl, beat together egg, flour, salt and pepper. Add shredded potatoes, zucchini and carrots; mix well. Oil 2 nonstick baking sheets. Drop heaping tablespoonfuls of vegetable mixture, 2 inches apart, onto baking sheets; flatten to make pancakes. Bake 8 to 15 minutes until bottoms are browned. Turn and bake 5 to 10 minutes more. Stir together sour cream and desired herbs or seasonings. Serve pancakes warm with dollop of herb cream.

Makes about 24 appetizer pancakes

Favorite recipe from **Colorado Potato Administrative Committee**

Spicy Marinated Shrimp

1 green onion, finely chopped

2 tablespoons olive oil

2 tablespoons fresh lemon juice

2 tablespoons prepared horseradish

2 tablespoons ketchup

1 tablespoon finely chopped chives

1 teaspoon TABASCO® brand Pepper Sauce

1 clove garlic, minced

1 teaspoon Dijon mustard

Salt to taste

2 pounds medium shrimp, cooked, peeled and deveined

Combine all ingredients except shrimp in large bowl. Add shrimp and toss to coat. Cover and refrigerate 4 to 6 hours or overnight. Transfer shrimp mixture to serving bowl and serve with toothpicks.

Makes 30 to 40 shrimp

Helpful Hint

To devein shrimp, use a sharp paring knife to cut a shallow slit down the back (outside curve) of the shrimp. Pull out the dark vein and rinse the shrimp under cold running water.

Spicy Marinated Shrimp

Gingered Chicken Pot Stickers

3 cups finely shredded cabbage

4 green onions with tops, finely chopped

1 egg white, lightly beaten

1 tablespoon light soy sauce

1 tablespoon minced fresh ginger

¼ teaspoon red pepper flakes

¼ pound ground chicken breast, cooked and drained

24 wonton wrappers, at room temperature

Cornstarch

½ cup water

1 tablespoon oyster sauce

2 teaspoons grated lemon peel

½ teaspoon honey

⅛ teaspoon crushed red pepper

1 tablespoon peanut oil

Steam cabbage 5 minutes, then cool to room temperature. Squeeze out any excess moisture; set aside. To prepare filling, combine green onions, egg white, soy sauce, ginger, ¼ teaspoon red pepper flakes in large bowl; blend well. Stir in cabbage and chicken.

To prepare pot stickers, place 1 tablespoon filling in center of 1 wonton wrapper. Gather edges around filling, pressing firmly at top to seal. Repeat with remaining wrappers and filling. Place pot stickers on large baking sheet dusted with cornstarch. Refrigerate 1 hour or until cold. Meanwhile, to prepare sauce, combine remaining ingredients except oil in small bowl; mix well. Set aside.

Heat oil in large nonstick skillet over high heat. Add pot stickers and cook until bottoms are golden brown. Pour sauce over top. Cover and cook 3 minutes. Uncover and cook until all liquid is absorbed. Serve warm on tray as finger food or on small plates with chopsticks as first course.

Makes 8 appetizer servings

Gingered Chicken Pot Stickers

Baked Cream Cheese Appetizer

Prep Time: 10 minutes   **Bake Time:** 18 minutes

1 can (4 ounces) refrigerated crescent dinner rolls

1 package (8 ounces) PHILADELPHIA® Cream Cheese

½ teaspoon dill weed

1 egg white, beaten

UNROLL dough on lightly greased cookie sheet; firmly press perforations together to form 12×4-inch rectangle.

SPRINKLE cream cheese with dill; lightly press dill into cream cheese. Place cream cheese, dill-side up, in center of dough. Bring edges of dough up over cream cheese; press edges of dough together to seal, completely enclosing cream cheese. Brush with egg white.

BAKE at 350°F for 15 to 18 minutes or until lightly browned. Serve with NABISCO® Crackers, French bread or fresh fruit slices.

Makes 8 servings

Great Substitutes: Substitute combined ½ teaspoon dried rosemary leaves, crushed, and ½ teaspoon paprika for the dill weed.

Helpful Hint

Fresh dill has beautiful feathery green leaves and can grow to a height of 3 feet. It can be found in some supermarkets and at farmer's markets in season—use it to create the perfect garnish for this simple appetizer.

Baked Cream Cheese Appetizer

Spicy Beef Turnovers

½ **pound lean ground beef or turkey**

2 **cloves garlic, minced**

2 **tablespoons soy sauce**

1 **tablespoon water**

½ **teaspoon cornstarch**

1 **teaspoon curry powder**

¼ **teaspoon Chinese five-spice powder**

¼ **teaspoon red pepper flakes**

2 **tablespoons minced green onion**

1 **package (7.5 ounces) refrigerated biscuits**

1 **egg**

1 **tablespoon water**

1. Preheat oven to 400°F. Cook beef with garlic in medium skillet over medium-high heat until beef is no longer pink, stirring to separate beef. Spoon off fat.

2. Blend soy sauce and water into cornstarch in cup until smooth. Add soy sauce mixture along with curry powder, five-spice powder and red pepper flakes to skillet. Cook and stir 30 seconds or until liquid is absorbed, stirring constantly. Remove from heat; stir in onion.

3. Roll each biscuit between 2 sheets of waxed paper into 4-inch rounds. Spoon heaping 1 tablespoon beef mixture onto one side of each biscuit; fold over, forming a semi-circle. Pinch edges together to seal.*

4. Arrange turnovers on baking sheet coated with nonstick cooking spray. Beat egg with water in cup; brush lightly over turnovers. Bake 9 to 10 minutes until golden brown. Serve warm or at room temperature. *Makes 10 appetizers*

At this point, turnovers may be wrapped and frozen up to 3 months. Thaw completely before proceeding as directed in step 4.

Bacon Appetizer Crescents

Prep Time: 30 minutes   **Bake Time:** 15 minutes

1 package (8 ounces) PHILADELPHIA® Cream Cheese, softened

½ cup OSCAR MAYER® Bacon Bits *or* 8 slices OSCAR MAYER® Bacon, crisply cooked, crumbled

⅓ cup KRAFT® 100% Grated Parmesan Cheese

¼ cup thinly sliced green onions

1 tablespoon milk

2 cans (8 ounces each) refrigerated crescent dinner rolls

Poppy seed (optional)

MIX cream cheese, bacon bits, Parmesan cheese, onions and milk until well blended.

SEPARATE dough into 8 rectangles; firmly press perforations together to seal. Spread each rectangle with 2 rounded tablespoonfuls cream cheese mixture.

CUT each rectangle in half diagonally; repeat with opposite corners. Cut in half crosswise to form 6 triangles. Roll up triangles, starting at short ends. Place on ungreased cookie sheets. Sprinkle with poppy seed.

BAKE at 375°F for 12 to 15 minutes or until golden brown. Serve immediately.   *Makes 4 dozen*

Cheesy Mushroom Crostini

Prep Time: 20 minutes   **Cook Time:** about 25 minutes

1 small loaf French bread, sliced ½ inch thick

1½ tablespoons butter, melted

1 tablespoon olive oil

1 package (10 ounces) mushrooms, wiped clean and sliced

2 tablespoons dry sherry

1 clove garlic, minced

1 teaspoon Italian seasoning

½ teaspoon salt

1⅓ cups *French's*® *Taste Toppers*™ French Fried Onions

1 cup (4 ounces) shredded Monterey Jack cheese

¼ cup grated Parmesan cheese

Preheat oven to 350°F. Place bread slices on baking sheet; brush with melted butter. Bake 10 to 15 minutes or until golden brown. Set aside.

Heat oil in large nonstick skillet over medium-high heat. Add mushrooms; cook and stir 5 minutes. Add sherry, garlic, Italian seasoning and salt; cook and stir 3 minutes or until liquid is evaporated and mushrooms are golden.

Spoon mixture evenly over bread. Layer with *Taste Toppers* and cheeses, beginning and ending with *Taste Toppers*. Bake 5 to 8 minutes or until cheese is melted and *Taste Toppers* are golden. Serve warm.

Makes about 7 appetizer servings

Cheesy Mushroom Crostini

Spicy Orange Chicken Kabob Appetizers

2 boneless, skinless chicken breast halves

1 small red or green bell pepper

24 small fresh button mushrooms

½ cup orange juice

2 tablespoons reduced-sodium soy sauce

1 tablespoon vegetable oil

1½ teaspoons onion powder

½ teaspoon Chinese five-spice powder

1. Cut chicken and pepper each into 24 (¾-inch) square pieces. Place chicken, pepper and mushrooms in large resealable plastic food storage bag. Combine juice, soy sauce, oil, onion powder and five-spice powder in small bowl. Pour over chicken mixture. Close bag securely; turn to coat. Marinate in refrigerator 4 to 24 hours, turning frequently.

2. Soak 24 small wooden skewers or toothpicks in water 30 minutes. Meanwhile, preheat broiler. Coat broiler pan with nonstick cooking spray.

3. Drain chicken, pepper and mushrooms, reserving marinade. Place marinade in small saucepan; bring to a full boil. Thread 1 piece chicken, 1 piece pepper and 1 mushroom onto each skewer. Place on prepared pan. Brush with marinade; discard remaining marinade. Broil 4 inches from heat source 5 to 6 minutes until chicken is no longer pink in center. Serve immediately. *Makes 24 servings*

Spicy Orange Chicken Kabob Appetizers

Spinach Cheese Triangles

Prep Time: 30 minutes   **Bake Time:** 15 minutes

1 package (8 ounces)
   PHILADELPHIA® Cream
   Cheese, softened

1 package (10 ounces) frozen
   chopped spinach,
   thawed, well drained

⅓ cup chopped drained
   roasted red peppers

¼ teaspoon garlic salt

6 sheets frozen phyllo,
   thawed

½ cup (1 stick) butter or
   margarine, melted

MIX cream cheese, spinach, red peppers and garlic salt with electric mixer on medium speed until well blended.

LAY 1 phyllo sheet on flat surface. Brush with some of the melted butter. Cut lengthwise into 4 (18×3½-inch) strips.

SPOON about 1 tablespoon filling about 1 inch from one end of each strip. Fold the end over the filling at a 45-degree angle. Continue folding as you would fold a flag to form a triangle that encloses filling. Repeat procedure with remaining phyllo sheets. Place triangles on cookie sheet. Brush with melted butter.

BAKE at 375°F for 12 to 15 minutes or until golden brown.

Makes 2 dozen appetizers

Tip: Unfold phyllo sheets; cover with wax paper and damp towel to prevent drying until ready to use.

Helpful Hint

Thaw frozen phyllo sheets overnight in the refrigerator. Once opened, phyllo should be used within a few days. (It cannot be refrozen.)

Pineapple-Scallop Bites

Prep Time: 25 minutes   **Cook Time:** 6 minutes

½ cup *French's*® Dijon Mustard

¼ cup orange marmalade

1 cup canned pineapple cubes (24 pieces)

12 sea scallops (8 ounces), cut in half crosswise

12 strips (6 ounces) uncooked turkey bacon, cut in half crosswise*

*Or substitute regular bacon for turkey bacon. Simmer 5 minutes in enough boiling water to cover; drain well before wrapping scallops.

1. Soak 12 (6-inch) bamboo skewers in hot water 20 minutes. Combine mustard and marmalade in small bowl. Reserve ½ cup mixture for dipping sauce.

2. Hold 1 pineapple cube and 1 scallop half together. Wrap with 1 bacon strip. Thread onto skewer. Repeat with remaining pineapple, scallops and bacon.

3. Place skewers on oiled grid. Grill over medium heat 6 minutes, turning frequently and brushing with remaining mustard mixture. Serve hot with reserved dipping sauce.   *Makes 6 servings*

Shrimp Quesadillas

½ cup ricotta cheese

1 medium green onion, sliced

2 tablespoons TABASCO® brand Green Pepper Sauce, divided

4 (7-inch) flour tortillas

8 ounces shrimp, cooked and chopped

1 small tomato, chopped

½ cup (2 ounces) shredded Muenster cheese

Preheat oven to 450°F. Combine ricotta cheese, green onion and 1 tablespoon TABASCO® Green Pepper Sauce in small bowl. Spread on 2 tortillas; sprinkle with half of chopped shrimp. Top with remaining tortillas.

Top tortillas with remaining shrimp, tomato and cheese; sprinkle with remaining 1 tablespoon TABASCO® Green Pepper Sauce. Bake 5 to 8 minutes or until cheese is melted. To serve, cut into wedges.

Makes 4 appetizer servings

Onion and Pepper Calzones

Prep and Cook Time: 25 minutes

1 teaspoon vegetable oil

½ cup chopped onion

½ cup chopped green bell pepper

¼ teaspoon salt

⅛ teaspoon dried basil leaves

⅛ teaspoon dried oregano leaves

⅛ teaspoon black pepper

1 can (12 ounces) country biscuits (10 biscuits)

¼ cup (1 ounce) shredded mozzarella cheese

½ cup prepared spaghetti or pizza sauce

2 tablespoons grated Parmesan cheese

1. Preheat oven to 400°F. Heat oil in medium nonstick skillet over medium-high heat. Add onion and bell pepper. Cook 5 minutes, stirring occasionally. Remove from heat. Add salt, basil, oregano and black pepper; stir to combine. Cool slightly.

2. While onion mixture is cooling, flatten biscuits into 3½-inch circles about ⅛ inch thick using palm of hand.

3. Stir mozzarella cheese into onion mixture; spoon 1 teaspoonful onto each biscuit. Fold biscuits in half, covering filling. Press edges with tines of fork to seal; transfer to baking sheet.

4. Bake 10 to 12 minutes or until golden brown. While calzones are baking, place spaghetti sauce in small microwavable bowl. Cover with vented plastic wrap. Microwave at HIGH 3 minutes or until hot.

5. To serve, spoon spaghetti sauce and Parmesan cheese evenly over each calzone. Serve immediately. *Makes 10 appetizers*

Onion and Pepper Calzones

Savory Sweetie Pies

2 tablespoons all-purpose flour

1 teaspoon dried rubbed sage

¼ teaspoon salt

¼ teaspoon black pepper

½ pound boneless, skinless chicken breasts, chopped

2 tablespoons butter or margarine

1 cup chicken broth

1 cup thawed frozen mixed vegetables

1 package (15 ounces) refrigerated pie crusts

1 egg yolk

1 teaspoon water

1. Preheat oven to 400°F. Lightly grease baking sheets.

2. Combine flour, sage, salt and pepper in medium bowl. Add chicken; toss to coat.

3. Melt butter in large skillet over medium heat. Add chicken and any remaining flour mixture; cook, stirring frequently, 5 minutes or until chicken is no longer pink in center. Stir in broth and vegetables. Reduce heat to low; simmer 5 to 8 minutes or until mixture is heated through.

4. On floured surface, roll 1 pie crust to 14-inch diameter. Cut out heart shapes using pattern or cookie cutter. Repeat with second pie crust, rerolling pastry if necessary, to get 30 hearts. Place half of hearts on prepared baking sheets; top each with heaping tablespoonful chicken mixture. Cover with remaining hearts; press edges together with fork to seal.

5. Combine egg yolk and water in small bowl; mix until well blended. Brush onto hearts.

6. Bake 15 to 20 minutes or until golden brown.

Makes 15 appetizer servings

Waldorf Appetizer Pizzas

½ package (5 ounces) washed fresh spinach or frozen thawed spinach

½ red apple, cored

1 tablespoon lemon juice

Nonstick cooking spray

¼ cup (1 ounce) chopped walnuts

2 large cloves garlic, minced

2 tablespoons golden raisins

1 teaspoon olive oil

2 packages (8 ounces each) 6-inch Italian bread shell

¼ cup (1 ounce) crumbled Gorgonzola cheese or blue cheese

Black pepper

1. Preheat oven to 450°F. Remove and discard stems from spinach. Rinse leaves and drain well; set aside. Thinly slice apple, cut slices into ½-inch pieces. Place in small bowl with lemon juice and 1 tablespoon water; stir to completely coat apple pieces with juice. Drain; set aside.

2. Spray large skillet with cooking spray. Heat over medium-high heat until hot. Add walnuts; cook and stir 5 to 6 minutes or until nuts are light golden. Stir in apple, garlic and raisins. Add spinach and drizzle with olive oil. Cover and cook 1 minute or until spinach begins to wilt. Stir until spinach is just wilted and coated with oil.

3. Place bread shells on baking sheet. Divide spinach mixture evenly among shells, leaving ½-inch border. Crumble cheese over spinach. Sprinkle with pepper. Bake 6 minutes or until cheese is melted and shells are warm. Cut each shell into 4 wedges.

Makes 8 servings (2 pieces each)

Spinach-Artichoke Party Cups

36 small wonton wrappers
(2 ½ to 3 ½ inches
square)

1 small can (8½ ounces)
artichoke hearts, drained
and chopped

½ package (10 ounces) frozen
chopped spinach, thawed
and well drained

1 cup shredded Monterey
Jack cheese

½ cup grated Parmesan
cheese

½ cup mayonnaise

1 clove garlic, minced

Preheat oven to 325°F. Spray mini muffin pan lightly with nonstick cooking spray. Press one wonton wrapper into each cup; spray lightly with cooking spray. Bake about 9 minutes or until light golden brown. Remove shells from muffin pan and set aside to cool. Repeat with remaining wonton wrappers.*

Meanwhile, combine artichoke hearts, spinach, cheeses, mayonnaise and garlic in medium bowl; mix well.

Fill wonton cups with spinach-artichoke mixture (about 2 teaspoons). Place filled cups on baking sheet. Bake about 7 minutes or until heated through. Serve immediately

Makes 36 appetizers

Wonton cups may be prepared up to one week in advance. Cool completely and store in an airtight container.

Tip: If you have leftover spinach-artichoke mixture after filling the wonton cups, place it in a shallow ovenproof dish and bake it at 350°F until hot and bubbly. Serve with bread or crackers.

Spinach-Artichoke Party Cups

Southern Crab Cakes with Rémoulade Dipping Sauce

10 ounces fresh lump
    crabmeat

1½ cups fresh white or
    sourdough bread
    crumbs, divided

¼ cup chopped green onions

½ cup mayonnaise, divided

1 egg white, lightly beaten

2 tablespoons coarse grain
    or spicy brown mustard,
    divided

¾ teaspoon hot pepper
    sauce, divided

2 teaspoons olive oil, divided

Lemon wedges

1. Preheat oven to 200°F. Combine crabmeat, ¾ cup bread crumbs and green onions in medium bowl. Add ¼ cup mayonnaise, egg white, 1 tablespoon mustard and ½ teaspoon pepper sauce; mix well. Using ¼ cup mixture per cake, shape eight ½-inch-thick cakes. Roll crab cakes lightly in remaining ¾ cup bread crumbs.

2. Heat large nonstick skillet over medium heat until hot; add 1 teaspoon oil. Add 4 crab cakes; cook 4 to 5 minutes per side or until golden brown. Transfer to serving platter; keep warm in oven. Repeat with remaining 1 teaspoon oil and crab cakes.

3. To prepare dipping sauce, combine remaining ¼ cup mayonnaise, 1 tablespoon mustard and ¼ teaspoon hot pepper sauce in small bowl; mix well.

4. Serve crab cakes warm with lemon wedges and dipping sauce.

Makes 8 servings

Helpful Hint

To make fresh bread crumbs, toast slices of bread very lightly, then place them in a food processor. Process with on/off pulses until the crumbs are the desired texture. One slice of bread will make about ½ cup fresh bread crumbs.

Southern Crab Cakes with Rémoulade Dipping Sauce

Strawberry Champagne Punch

Prep Time: 15 minutes

2 packages (10 ounces each) frozen sliced strawberries in syrup, thawed

2 cans (5½ ounces each) apricot or peach nectar

¼ cup lemon juice

2 tablespoons honey

2 bottles (750 ml each) champagne or sparkling white wine, chilled

1. Place strawberries with syrup in food processor; process until smooth.

2. Pour puréed strawberries into large punch bowl. Stir in apricot nectar, lemon juice and honey; blend well. Refrigerate until serving time.

3. To serve, stir champagne into strawberry mixture.

Makes 12 servings

Tip: To save time, thaw the strawberries in the refrigerator the day before using them.

Piquant Veracruz Clams

6 clams, opened*

2 ounces bacon bits

1 tablespoon ROSE'S® Lime Juice

3 ounces butter, slightly soft

¼ cup seasoned breadcrumbs

Salt and black pepper

Ask your seafood supplier to provide you with the clam meat and their shells separately.

1. Preheat oven to 350°F. In a bowl, mix clam meat, bacon bits, lime juice, butter and breadcrumbs. Season to taste with salt and pepper.

2. Fill each clam shell with mixture and place on baking sheet in oven for 6 to 8 minutes, or until filling turns golden brown.

Makes 2 servings (3 clams each)

Strawberry Champagne Punch

Holiday Cheer

Marinated Roasted Pepper Tapas

1 large red bell pepper

1 large yellow bell pepper

3 tablespoons olive oil

1 tablespoon sherry wine vinegar or white wine vinegar

1 tablespoon capers, rinsed and drained

1 teaspoon sugar

1 clove garlic, sliced

½ teaspoon cumin seeds

1 loaf French bread

1. Cover broiler pan with foil. Preheat broiler. Place peppers on foil. Broil, 4 inches from heat source, 15 to 20 minutes or until blackened on all sides, turning peppers every 5 minutes with tongs. Place peppers in paper bag for 30 minutes.

2. Place oil, vinegar, capers, sugar, garlic and cumin seeds in small bowl. Whisk until combined.

3. Peel, core and seed peppers; cut into 1-inch diamond or square-shaped pieces. Place in resealable plastic food storage bag. Pour oil mixture over peppers. Cover and refrigerate at least 2 hours or overnight, turning occasionally. Bring to room temperature before serving.

4. Slice bread into rounds; toast, if desired. Arrange peppers on top of rounds.

Makes 4 to 6 appetizer servings

Marinated Roasted Pepper Tapas

Savory Onion Focaccia

Prep Time: 30 minutes   **Cook Time:** 27 minutes

1 pound frozen pizza or
   bread dough*

1 tablespoon olive oil

1 clove garlic, minced

1⅓ cups *French's®* *Taste*
   Toppers™ French Fried
   Onions, divided

1 cup (4 ounces) shredded
   mozzarella cheese

½ pound plum tomatoes
   (4 small), thinly sliced

2 teaspoons fresh chopped
   rosemary *or* ½ teaspoon
   dried rosemary

3 tablespoons grated
   Parmesan cheese

**Pizza dough may be found in frozen
section of supermarket. Thaw in
refrigerator before using.*

Bring pizza dough to room temperature. Grease 15×10-inch
jelly-roll pan. Roll or pat dough into rectangle same size as pan
on floured board.** Transfer dough to pan.

Combine oil and garlic in small bowl; brush onto surface of dough.
Cover loosely with kitchen towel. Let dough rise at room
temperature 25 minutes. Prick dough with fork.

Preheat oven to 450°F. Bake dough 20 minutes or until edges
and bottom of crust are golden. Sprinkle *1 cup* **Taste Toppers** and
mozzarella cheese over dough. Arrange tomatoes over cheese;
sprinkle with rosemary. Bake 5 minutes or until cheese melts.

Sprinkle with remaining *⅓ cup* **Taste Toppers** and Parmesan cheese.
Bake 2 minutes or until **Taste Toppers** are golden. To serve, cut into
rectangles.   *Makes 8 appetizer servings*

**If dough is too hard to roll, allow to rest on floured board.

Savory Onion Focaccia

Christmas Confetti Dip

1 cup sour cream

4 teaspoons dry ranch-style
salad dressing mix

¼ cup finely chopped carrot

¼ cup finely chopped
cucumber

¼ cup finely chopped red bell
pepper

¼ cup finely chopped zucchini

1. Combine sour cream and dressing mix in medium bowl; mix well. Stir in chopped vegetables; cover. Refrigerate 2 to 3 hours for flavors to blend.

2. Transfer dip to medium serving bowl. Garnish with bell pepper cutouts, if desired. Serve with assorted fresh vegetable dippers.

Makes 8 (¼-cup) servings

Dilly of a Dip: Substitute ½ cup finely chopped seeded cucumber for the 1 cup finely chopped vegetables listed above. Stir in 1 to 1½ teaspoons dill weed or dried basil leaves, crushed. Makes about 1¾ cups.

Fresh Veggie Spread: Beat 1½ (8-ounce) packages softened cream cheese in medium bowl until creamy. Beat in enough sour cream to make desired consistency for spreading. Stir in 3 to 4 tablespoons each chopped red bell pepper, zucchini and carrot. Stir in 1 to 1½ teaspoons dill weed or dried oregano leaves, crushed. Spread onto assorted crackers or party rye bread slices. Makes about 2 cups.

Quick Veggie Spread: Prepare Fresh Veggie Spread, substituting ¼ cup dry vegetable soup mix for the chopped fresh vegetables. Makes about 1½ cups.

Pesto Cheese Wreath

Parsley-Basil Pesto* (recipe follows)

3 packages (8 ounces each) cream cheese, softened

½ cup mayonnaise

¼ cup whipping cream or half-and-half

1 teaspoon sugar

1 teaspoon onion salt

⅓ cup chopped roasted red peppers** or pimiento, drained

Pimiento strips and Italian flat leaf parsley leaves (optional)

Assorted crackers and cut-up vegetables

*One-half cup purchased pesto may be substituted for Parsley-Basil Pesto.

**Look for roasted red peppers packed in cans or jars in the Italian food section of the supermarket.

Prepare Parsley-Basil Pesto. Beat cream cheese and mayonnaise in medium bowl until smooth; beat in cream, sugar and onion salt.

Line 5-cup ring mold with plastic wrap. Spoon half of cheese mixture into prepared mold; spread evenly. Spread Parsley-Basil Pesto evenly over cheese mixture; top with chopped red peppers. Spoon remaining cheese mixture over peppers; spread evenly. Cover; refrigerate until cheese mixture is firm, 8 hours or overnight.

Uncover mold; invert onto serving plate. Carefully remove plastic wrap. Smooth top and sides of wreath with spatula. Garnish with pimiento strips and parsley leaves, if desired. Serve with assorted crackers and vegetables.   *Makes 16 to 24 appetizer servings*

Parsley-Basil Pesto

2 cups fresh parsley leaves

¼ cup pine nuts or slivered almonds

2 tablespoons grated Parmesan cheese

2 cloves garlic, peeled

1 tablespoon dried basil leaves, crushed

¼ teaspoon salt

2 tablespoons olive or vegetable oil

Process all ingredients except oil in food processor or blender until finely chopped. With machine running, add oil gradually, processing until mixture is smooth.   *Makes about ½ cup*

Cranberry-Glazed Brie

Cornmeal

¾ cup canned whole berry cranberry sauce, well drained

¼ teaspoon dry mustard

⅛ teaspoon ground ginger

⅛ teaspoon ground cloves

⅛ teaspoon ground allspice

1 package (17¼ ounces) frozen puff pastry sheets, thawed

1 round (15 ounces) fully ripened Brie cheese

1 egg

1 tablespoon water

Green, red and yellow food colors

Sliced pears and/or assorted crackers

1. Preheat oven to 400°F. Lightly sprinkle baking sheet with cornmeal. Mix cranberry sauce, dry mustard and spices.

2. Place 1 puff pastry sheet on lightly floured surface; roll out pastry with rolling pin about 2 inches larger than diameter of cheese round. Place cheese in center of pastry. Cut away excess pastry with sharp knife, leaving 1-inch rim around bottom of cheese; reserve trimmings. Place on prepared baking sheet. Spread cranberry mixture onto top of cheese to within 1 inch of edge.

3. Roll out remaining pastry sheet to a size large enough to cover cheese completely. Place pastry over cheese; trim away excess pastry. (Be sure to leave 1-inch rim of pastry at bottom of cheese.) Cut slits in top of pastry with sharp knife to allow steam to vent.

4. Combine egg and water; beat lightly with fork. Brush onto pastry to cover completely. Fold up bottom rim of pastry; press edges together to seal.

5. Cut out leaves or other decorative designs from pastry trimmings. Attach cutouts to top pastry with remaining egg mixture; brush with food colors that have been diluted slightly with water.

6. Bake 15 minutes. Reduce oven temperature to 350°F. Continue baking 15 to 20 minutes or until pastry is golden brown. Remove to wire rack; let stand 15 minutes before cutting to serve. Serve warm with pear slices or crackers. *Makes 12 appetizer servings*

Cranberry-Glazed Brie

Holiday Meatballs

1½ pounds lean ground beef

⅔ cup dry bread crumbs

1 egg, slightly beaten

¼ cup water

3 tablespoons minced onion

1 clove garlic, minced

½ teaspoon salt

¼ teaspoon pepper

1 tablespoon vegetable oil

1 cup HEINZ® Chili Sauce

1 cup grape jelly

Combine first 8 ingredients. Form into 60 bite-sized meatballs using rounded teaspoon for each. Place in shallow baking pan or jelly-roll pan brushed with oil. Bake in 450°F oven 15 minutes or until cooked through. Meanwhile, in small saucepan, combine chili sauce and grape jelly. Heat until jelly is melted. Place well-drained meatballs in serving dish. Pour chili sauce mixture over; stir gently to coat. Serve warm. *Makes 60 appetizers*

Tip: For a zestier sauce, substitute hot jalapeno jelly for grape jelly.

Cocktail Wraps

16 thin strips Cheddar cheese*

16 HILLSHIRE FARM® Lit'l Smokies, scored lengthwise into halves

1 can (8 ounces) refrigerated crescent roll dough

1 egg, beaten *or* 1 tablespoon milk

Mustard

Or substitute Swiss, taco-flavored or other variety of cheese.

Preheat oven to 400°F.

Place 1 strip cheese inside score of each Lit'l Smokie. Separate dough into 8 triangles; cut each lengthwise into halves to make 16 triangles. Place 1 link on wide end of 1 dough triangle; roll up. Repeat with remaining links and dough triangles. Place links on baking sheet. Brush dough with egg. Bake 10 to 15 minutes.

Serve hot with mustard. *Makes 16 hors d'oeuvres*

Marinated Citrus Shrimp

1 pound (about 32) large shrimp, peeled, tails left intact and cooked

2 oranges, peeled and cut into segments

1 can (5 ½ ounces) pineapple chunks in juice, drained and ¼ cup juice reserved

2 green onions with tops, sliced

½ cup orange juice

2 tablespoons minced fresh cilantro

2 tablespoons lime juice

2 tablespoons white wine vinegar

1 tablespoon olive or vegetable oil

1 clove garlic, minced

½ teaspoon dried basil leaves

½ teaspoon dried tarragon leaves

White pepper (optional)

1. Combine shrimp, orange segments, pineapple chunks and green onions in resealable plastic food storage bag. Mix orange juice, reserved pineapple juice, cilantro, lime juice, vinegar, oil, garlic, basil and tarragon in medium bowl; pour over shrimp mixture, turning to coat. Season to taste with white pepper, if desired. Marinate in refrigerator 2 hours or up to 8 hours.

2. Spoon shrimp mixture onto plates. Garnish, if desired.

Makes 16 servings

Cheese Pine Cones

2 cups (8 ounces) shredded Swiss cheese

½ cup butter or margarine, softened

3 tablespoons milk

2 tablespoons dry sherry or milk

⅛ teaspoon ground red pepper

1 cup finely chopped blanched almonds

¾ cup slivered blanched almonds

¾ cup sliced almonds

½ cup whole almonds

Fresh rosemary sprigs

Assorted crackers

Beat cheese, butter, milk, sherry and red pepper in medium bowl until smooth; stir in chopped almonds.

Divide mixture into 3 equal portions; shape each into tapered ovals to resemble pine cones. Insert slivered, sliced and whole almonds into cones. Cover; refrigerate 2 to 3 hours or until firm.

Arrange Cheese Pine Cones on wooden board or serving plate. Garnish tops with rosemary. Serve with assorted crackers.

Makes 12 to 16 appetizer servings

Helpful Hint

To soften a stick of butter quickly, place it on a microwavable plate and heat at LOW (30% power) about 30 seconds or just until softened.

Cheese Pine Cones

Holiday Star

TOPPING

¾ cup sour cream

½ cup mayonnaise

2 tablespoons heavy cream

1 teaspoon balsamic vinegar

¼ cup chopped fresh cilantro

¼ cup chopped fresh basil

¼ cup chopped roasted red peppers, drained and patted dry

½ teaspoon garlic powder

¼ teaspoon salt

Black pepper to taste

STAR

2 cans (8 ounces each) refrigerated crescent roll dough

GARNISHES

Red bell pepper, chopped

Green onion, chopped

Black olive slices (optional)

1. Preheat oven to 375°F. Combine sour cream, mayonnaise, heavy cream and balsamic vinegar in medium bowl. Stir in cilantro, basil and roasted red peppers. Add garlic powder, salt and black pepper; mix well. Cover and refrigerate at least 1 hour.

2. Place 2-inch round cookie cutter or similar size custard cup in center of 14-inch pizza pan; set aside. Remove dough from first can and unroll on cookie sheet. Seal perforations by pressing down slightly with fingers. Cut 24 circles with 1½-inch cookie cutter; reserve excess dough. Repeat with second can.

3. Evenly space five dough circles around the outside edge of the pizza pan. (These will be the star points.) From each star point, make a triangle pattern with rows of slightly overlapping dough circles, working toward the cookie cutter in center of pan. Roll excess dough into a ball; flatten with hands. Cut more circles as needed to completely fill star.

4. Remove cookie cutter in center of star. Bake 12 to 16 minutes or until star is light golden brown. Cool completely in pan on wire rack, about 30 minutes.

5. Spread topping over star. Garnish with red bell pepper, green onion and black olives, if desired. Place decorative candle in center of star. Serve immediately. *Makes about 16 servings*

Helpful Hint: For a festive garnish, hollow out a red or green bell pepper and fill it with any remaining dip. Place fresh vegetables, such as broccoli florets or bell pepper strips, around the star.

Holiday Star

Tomato-Pesto Stuffed Brie

Prep Time: 30 minutes   **Chill Time:** 1 hour

1 cup boiling water

1 package (3 ounces) unsalted sun-dried tomatoes (about 2 cups)

4 tablespoons *Frank's®* *RedHot®* Cayenne Pepper Sauce

2 green onions, chopped

2 (5-inch) whole Brie, about 13 ounces each, well chilled

1 jar (1¾ ounces) pine nuts, toasted*

3 tablespoons butter, softened

¾ cup chopped fresh parsley

*To toast pine nuts, bake at 350°F 5 minutes or until golden.

1. Pour boiling water over tomatoes in medium bowl. Let stand 4 minutes or until just softened; drain well and pat dry with paper towels. Place tomatoes, *Frank's RedHot* and onions in food processor; process until smooth paste forms.

2. Using large sharp knife, split each Brie round in half horizontally. Spread tomato mixture over cut sides of bottom halves. Sprinkle evenly with pine nuts. Cover bottom halves with top halves, cut side down. Press gently. Spread butter on edges of rounds; roll in chopped parsley. Refrigerate about 1 hour. Cut into wedges; serve with crackers or French bread. *Makes 12 servings*

Tip: Filled Brie may be served warm. (Do not coat with butter and parsley.) Place in baking dish; bake at 325°F 5 to 10 minutes or until slightly softened.

Tomato-Pesto Stuffed Brie

Mushroom Bruschetta

Prep and Cook Time: 23 minutes

1 clove garlic

½ cup chopped mushrooms

2 tablespoons chopped red bell pepper

1 green onion, thinly sliced

1 tablespoon grated Parmesan cheese, divided

1 tablespoon olive or vegetable oil

½ teaspoon lemon juice

¼ teaspoon dried tarragon leaves

¼ teaspoon dried thyme leaves

6 slices French bread (½ inch thick)

1. Preheat broiler. Peel garlic clove and cut in half. Mince one half; set other half aside.

2. Combine mushrooms, bell pepper, green onion, minced garlic, 1½ teaspoons Parmesan, oil, lemon juice, tarragon and thyme in small bowl. Add salt and pepper to taste.

3. Arrange bread slices on cookie sheet. Broil 4 inches from heat source 2 to 3 minutes per side or until lightly browned.

4. Remove cookie sheet from broiler; rub tops of bread with cut side of reserved garlic. Spoon about 1 tablespoon mushroom mixture on each bread slice and sprinkle with remaining 1½ teaspoons Parmesan. Broil 1 to 2 minutes or until cheese is melted. Serve warm.

Makes 2 servings

Holiday Meat and Vegetable Kabobs

1 cup fresh pearl onions

⅓ cup olive oil

2 tablespoons balsamic vinegar

1 tablespoon TABASCO® brand Pepper Sauce

1 tablespoon dried basil leaves

2 large cloves garlic, crushed

1 teaspoon salt

1 pound boneless skinless chicken breasts

1 pound boneless beef sirloin

2 large red peppers, cored, seeded and cut into ¾-inch pieces

1 large green pepper, cored, seeded and cut into ¾-inch pieces

1 large zucchini, cut into ¾-inch pieces

Soak 3 dozen 4-inch-long wooden skewers in water overnight. Bring pearl onions and enough water to cover in 1-quart saucepan over high heat to a boil. Reduce heat to low. Cover and simmer 3 minutes or until onions are tender. Drain. When cool enough to handle, peel away outer layer of skin from onions.

Combine oil, vinegar, TABASCO® Sauce, basil, garlic and salt in medium bowl. Pour half of mixture into another bowl. Cut chicken and beef into ¾-inch pieces and place in bowl with TABASCO® Sauce mixture, tossing well to coat. In remaining bowl of TABASCO® Sauce mixture, toss pearl onions, red and green peppers and zucchini. Let stand at least 30 minutes, tossing occasionally.

Preheat broiler. Skewer 1 piece of chicken or beef and 1 piece each of red pepper, green pepper, onion and zucchini onto each wooden pick. Broil 4 to 6 minutes, turning occasionally.

Makes 3 dozen hors d'oeuvres

Cranberry-Orange Snack Mix

2 cups oatmeal cereal
squares

2 cups corn cereal squares

2 cups mini pretzels

1 cup whole almonds

¼ cup butter

⅓ cup frozen orange juice
concentrate, thawed

3 tablespoons packed brown
sugar

1 teaspoon ground cinnamon

¾ teaspoon ground ginger

¼ teaspoon ground nutmeg

⅔ cup dried cranberries

1. Preheat oven to 250°F. Spray 13×9-inch baking pan with nonstick cooking spray.

2. Combine cereal squares, pretzels and almonds in large bowl.

3. Melt butter in medium microwavable bowl at HIGH 45 to 60 seconds. Stir in orange juice concentrate, brown sugar, cinnamon, ginger and nutmeg until blended. Pour over cereal mixture; stir well to coat. Place in prepared pan and spread in single layer.

4. Bake 50 minutes, stirring every 10 minutes. Stir in cranberries. Let cool in pan on wire rack, leaving uncovered until mixture is crisp. Store in airtight container or resealable plastic food storage bags.

Makes 8 cups snack mix

Festive Stuffed Dates

Prep Time: 25 minutes

1 box (8 ounces) DOLE®
Whole Pitted Dates

1 package (3 ounces)
reduced fat cream
cheese, softened

¼ cup powdered sugar

1 tablespoon grated peel of
1 orange

• Make slit in center of each date. Combine cream cheese, powdered sugar and orange peel. Fill centers of dates with cream cheese mixture. Refrigerate.

• Dust with additional powdered sugar just before serving, if desired.

Makes about 27 stuffed dates

Cranberry-Orange Snack Mix

Festive Crab Toasts

1 can (10¾ ounces) condensed cream of celery soup

12 ounces crabmeat, flaked

¼ cup chopped celery

¼ cup sliced green onions

1 tablespoon lemon juice

⅛ teaspoon grated lemon peel

1 (8-ounce) French bread baguette

⅓ cup grated Parmesan cheese

Paprika

Combine soup, crabmeat, celery, onions, lemon juice and lemon peel in medium bowl; mix well. Cut baguette diagonally into ½-inch slices; arrange slices on 2 ungreased baking sheets. Broil 5 inches from heat 2 minutes until toasted, turning once.

Spread 1 tablespoon crab mixture on each baguette slice. Top with Parmesan cheese; sprinkle with paprika. Broil 5 inches from heat 2 minutes or until lightly browned.   *Makes about 30 appetizers*

Helpful Hint

You can get more juice from room-temperature lemons than from cold ones. Rolling lemons on the countertop while pressing down with your hand will also help release more juice from the lemons. One medium lemon will yield about 3 tablespoons juice and 2 to 3 teaspoons grated peel.

Festive Crab Toasts

Cheesy Christmas Trees

½ cup mayonnaise

1 tablespoon dry ranch-style
    salad dressing mix

1 cup shredded Cheddar
    cheese

¼ cup grated Parmesan
    cheese

12 slices firm white bread

¼ cup red bell pepper strips

¼ cup green bell pepper
    strips

1. Preheat broiler. Combine mayonnaise and salad dressing mix in medium bowl. Add cheeses; mix well.

2. Cut bread slices into Christmas tree shapes using large cookie cutters. Spread each tree with about 1 tablespoon mayonnaise mixture. Decorate with red and green bell pepper strips. Place on baking sheet.

3. Broil 4 inches from heat 2 to 3 minutes or until bubbling. Serve warm.

Makes about 12 appetizers

Brie Torte

1 (15- to 16-ounce) wheel
    Brie cheese

6 tablespoons butter,
    softened

⅓ cup chopped dried tart
    cherries

¼ cup finely chopped pecans

½ teaspoon dried thyme *or*
    2 teaspoons finely
    chopped fresh thyme

Refrigerate Brie until chilled and firm or freeze 30 minutes until firm. Cut Brie in half horizontally.

Combine butter, cherries, pecans and thyme in small bowl; mix well. Spread mixture evenly onto cut side of one half of Brie. Top with other half, cut side down. Lightly press together. Wrap in plastic wrap; refrigerate 1 to 2 hours. To serve, cut into serving size wedges and bring to room temperature. Serve with water crackers.

Makes about 20 appetizer servings

Note: If wrapped securely in plastic wrap, this appetizer will keep in the refrigerator for at least a week.

Favorite recipe from **Cherry Marketing Institute**

Praline Pecans & Cranberries

3½ cups pecan halves

¼ cup light corn syrup

¼ cup packed light brown sugar

2 tablespoons butter or margarine

1 teaspoon vanilla

¼ teaspoon baking soda

1½ cups dried cranberries or cherries

1. Preheat oven to 250°F. Grease 13×9-inch baking pan. Cover large baking sheet with heavy-duty aluminum foil.

2. Spread pecans in single layer in prepared baking pan.

3. Combine corn syrup, sugar and butter in small microwavable bowl. Microwave at HIGH 1 minute. Stir. Microwave 30 seconds to 1 minute or until boiling rapidly. Stir in vanilla and baking soda until well blended. Drizzle evenly over pecans; stir with wooden spoon until evenly coated.

4. Bake 1 hour, stirring every 20 minutes with wooden spoon. Immediately transfer mixture to prepared baking sheet, spreading pecans evenly over foil with lightly greased spatula.

5. Cool completely. Break pecans apart with wooden spoon. Combine pecans and cranberries in large bowl. Store in airtight container at room temperature up to 2 weeks.

Makes about 5 cups

East Meets West Cocktail Franks

1 cup prepared sweet and
  sour sauce

1½ tablespoons rice vinegar or
  cider vinegar

1 tablespoon grated fresh
  ginger *or* 1 teaspoon
  dried ginger

1 tablespoon dark sesame oil

½ teaspoon chile oil
  (optional)

1 package (12 ounces)
  HEBREW NATIONAL®
  Cocktail Beef Franks

2 tablespoons chopped
  cilantro or chives

Combine sweet and sour sauce, vinegar, ginger, sesame oil and chile oil in medium saucepan. Bring to a boil over medium heat. Cook 5 minutes or until thickened. Add cocktail franks; cover and cook until heated through. Transfer to chafing dish; sprinkle with cilantro. Serve with frilled wooden picks.

Makes 12 appetizer servings (2 cocktail franks per serving)

Helpful Hint

Rice vinegar is made from fermented rice and has a milder flavor than most Western vinegars. It can be found in Asian markets or the international section of many supermarkets.

East Meets West Cocktail Franks

Turkey Meatballs in Cranberry-Barbecue Sauce

1 can (16 ounces) jellied
    cranberry sauce

½ cup barbecue sauce

1 egg white

1 pound ground turkey

1 green onion with top, sliced

2 teaspoons grated orange
    peel

1 teaspoon reduced-sodium
    soy sauce

¼ teaspoon black pepper

⅛ teaspoon ground red
    pepper (optional)

Combine cranberry sauce and barbecue sauce in slow cooker. Cover and cook on HIGH 20 to 30 minutes or until cranberry sauce is melted and mixture is hot, stirring every 10 minutes.

Meanwhile, place egg white in medium bowl; beat lightly. Add turkey, green onion, orange peel, soy sauce, black pepper and ground red pepper, if desired; mix well with hands until well blended. Shape into 24 balls.

Spray large nonstick skillet with nonstick cooking spray. Add meatballs to skillet; cook over medium heat 8 to 10 minutes or until meatballs are no longer pink in center, carefully turning occasionally to brown evenly. Add to heated sauce in slow cooker; stir gently to coat evenly with sauce.

Reduce heat to LOW. Cover and cook 3 hours. When ready to serve, transfer meatballs to serving plate; garnish, if desired. Serve with decorative picks. *Makes 12 servings*

Turkey Meatballs in Cranberry-Barbecue Sauce

Party Cheese Wreath

Prep Time: 15 minutes plus refrigerating

2 packages (8 ounces each) PHILADELPHIA® Cream Cheese, softened

1 package (8 ounces) KRAFT® Shredded Sharp Cheddar Cheese

1 tablespoon *each* chopped red bell pepper and finely chopped onion

2 teaspoons Worcestershire sauce

1 teaspoon lemon juice

Dash ground red pepper

MIX cream cheese and Cheddar cheese with electric mixer on medium speed until well blended.

BLEND in remaining ingredients. Refrigerate several hours or overnight.

PLACE drinking glass in center of serving platter. Drop round tablespoonfuls of mixture around glass, just touching outer edge of glass to form ring; smooth with spatula. Remove glass. Garnish with chopped fresh parsley and chopped red pepper. Serve with NABISCO® Crackers. *Makes 12 servings*

Special Extra: Shape cream cheese mixture into 1-inch balls. Roll in light rye bread crumbs or dark pumpernickel bread crumbs.

Helpful Hint

To soften cream cheese in a hurry, place an unwrapped (8-ounce) package on a microwavable plate; heat at HIGH 15 seconds. Add 15 seconds for each additional package.

Party Cheese Wreath

Holiday Shrimp Dip

4½ teaspoons unflavored gelatin

¼ cup cold water

1 can (10¾ ounces) condensed tomato soup

1 (3-ounce) package cream cheese

1 cup mayonnaise

1 (6-ounce) bag frozen small shrimp, thawed

¾ cup finely chopped celery

2 tablespoons grated onion

¼ teaspoon salt

White pepper to taste

Bell peppers for garnish (optional)

Assorted crackers

1. Dissolve gelatin in cold water in small bowl; set aside. Grease four 1-cup holiday mold pans or one (5½-cup) holiday mold pan; set aside.

2. Heat soup in medium saucepan over medium heat until hot. Add cream cheese; blend well. Add gelatin mixture, mayonnaise, shrimp, celery, onion, and seasonings. Pour into prepared mold; refrigerate 30 minutes. Cover with foil and refrigerate overnight.

3. Decorate with bell peppers cut into holly leaves, if desired. Serve with assorted crackers. *Makes 12 servings*

Oregon Hot Apple Cider

8 cups apple cider

½ cup dried cherries

½ cup dried cranberries

3 cinnamon sticks, broken in half

8 whole cloves

1 pear, quartered, cored, sliced

1. Combine cider, cherries, cranberries, cinnamon and cloves in large saucepan. Heat just to a simmer; do not boil.

2. Add pear before serving. *Makes 16 (½ cup) servings*

Merry Crisps

1 cup all-purpose flour
½ teaspoon baking powder
½ teaspoon paprika
¼ teaspoon salt
⅓ cup plus 1 tablespoon water, divided
3 tablespoons vegetable oil
1 egg white
Toppings: seasoned salt, dried basil leaves or poppy seeds

1. Combine flour, baking powder, paprika and salt in medium bowl. Stir in ⅓ cup water and oil to form smooth dough; refrigerate 10 to 15 minutes.

2. Preheat oven to 400°F. Grease baking sheets.

3. Roll dough on floured surface to 14×12-inch rectangle. Cut out dough using 1- to 1½-inch holiday cookie cutters. Reroll scraps and cut into holiday shapes. Place on prepared baking sheets.

4. Combine egg white and remaining 1 tablespoon water; brush on crackers. Sprinkle with toppings as desired.

5. Bake 6 to 8 minutes or until edges begin to brown. Remove to wire rack; cool completely. *Makes 7½ dozen crackers*

Cranberry-Lime Margarita Punch

6 cups water
1 container (12 ounces) frozen cranberry juice cocktail
½ cup fresh lime juice
¼ cup sugar
2 cups ice cubes
1 cup ginger ale or tequila
1 lime, sliced

1. Combine water, cranberry juice, lime juice and sugar in punch bowl; stir until sugar dissolves.

2. Stir in ice cubes, ginger ale and lime; garnish with fresh cranberries, if desired. *Makes 10 (8-ounce) servings*

Festive Holiday Punch

8 cups MOTT'S® Apple Juice

8 cups cranberry juice cocktail

2 red apples, sliced

2 cups cranberries

3 liters lemon-lime soda

Ice cubes, as needed

Pour apple and cranberry juices into punch bowl. Fifteen minutes before serving, add apple slices, cranberries, soda and ice. Do not stir.

Makes 24 servings

Raspberry Eggnog

½ cup sugar

2 tablespoons cornstarch

4 cups skim milk, divided

2 eggs, beaten

1 package (12 ounces) frozen raspberries, thawed

1 teaspoon vanilla

6 to 9 drops red food coloring

Ground nutmeg

1. Combine sugar and cornstarch in large saucepan; stir in 2 cups milk. Bring to a boil over low heat, stirring constantly. Continue boiling 1 minute or until thickened, stirring constantly. Whisk small amount of hot milk mixture into eggs in small bowl. Whisk egg mixture back into hot milk mixture in saucepan. Cook over low heat 1 minute. Strain; cool.

2. Place raspberries in food processor or blender; process until smooth. Strain; discard seeds. Stir raspberry purée into milk mixture; stir in remaining 2 cups milk and vanilla. Add red food coloring, one drop at a time, until eggnog is desired shade. Cover; refrigerate until cold or ready to serve. Sprinkle each serving with nutmeg. Garnish with mint sprigs and raspberries, if desired.

Makes 12 (½-cup) servings

Festive Holiday Punch

Hot Mulled Cider

1 orange
1 lemon
12 whole cloves
6 cups apple cider
⅓ cup sugar
3 cinnamon sticks
12 whole allspice berries

Poke 6 evenly spaced holes around orange and lemon with point of wooden skewer. Insert whole cloves into holes. Cut slice out of orange to include all cloves. Cut remainder of orange into thin slices. Repeat procedure with lemon. Combine all ingredients in medium saucepan. Bring just to a simmer over medium heat. *Do not boil.* Reduce heat to low; cook 5 minutes. Pour cider through strainer into mugs. Discard fruit and seasonings. Garnish as desired.

Makes 6 cups

Christmas Carol Punch

2 medium red apples
2 quarts clear apple cider
½ cup SUN•MAID® Raisins
8 cinnamon sticks
2 teaspoons whole cloves
¼ cup lemon juice
Lemon slices
Orange slices

Core apples; slice into ½-inch rings. In Dutch oven, combine cider, apple rings, raisins, cinnamon and cloves. Bring to a boil over high heat; reduce heat to low and simmer 5 to 8 minutes or until apples are just tender. Remove cloves; add lemon juice, and lemon and orange slices. Pour into punch bowl. Ladle into large mugs, including an apple ring, some raisins and citrus slices in each serving. Serve with spoons.

Makes about 2 quarts

Hot Mulled Cider

Spiced Red Wine

Grape Ice Ring (recipe
  follows)
½ cup sugar
½ cup water
1 bottle (750 ml) Burgundy
  wine, chilled
2 cups white grape juice,
  chilled
1 cup peach schnapps, chilled

Prepare Grape Ice Ring.

Combine sugar and water in small saucepan. Bring to a boil. Boil, stirring constantly, until sugar dissolves. Cool to room temperature. Cover; refrigerate until chilled, about 2 hours.

Combine wine, grape juice, schnapps and sugar syrup in punch bowl. Float Grape Ice Ring in punch.   *Makes 14 servings*

Grape Ice Ring

2 pounds assorted seedless grapes (Thompson, Red Empress, etc.)
  Lemon leaves* (optional)

These nontoxic leaves are available in florist shops.

Fill 4-cup ring mold with water to within ¾ inch of top. Freeze until firm, about 8 hours or overnight. Arrange clusters of grapes and leaves on ice; fill with water to top of mold. Freeze until solid, about 6 hours. To unmold, dip bottom of mold briefly in hot water.

Makes 1 ring

Raspberry Wine Punch

1 package (10 ounces) frozen red raspberries in syrup, thawed

1 bottle (750 ml) white Zinfandel or blush wine

¼ cup raspberry-flavored liqueur

Empty ½ gallon milk or juice carton

3 to 4 cups distilled water, divided

Sprigs of pine and tinsel

Fresh cranberries

Process raspberries with syrup in food processor or blender until smooth; press through strainer, discarding seeds. Combine wine, raspberry purée and liqueur in pitcher; refrigerate until serving time. Rinse out wine bottle and remove label.

Fully open top of carton. Place wine bottle in center of carton. Tape bottle securely to carton so bottle will not move when adding water. Pour 2 cups distilled water into carton. Carefully push pine sprigs, cranberries and tinsel into water between bottle and carton to form decorative design. Add remaining water to almost fill carton. Freeze until firm, 8 hours or overnight.

Just before serving, peel carton from ice block. Using funnel, pour punch back into wine bottle. Wrap bottom of ice block with white cotton napkin or towel to hold while serving.   *Makes 8 servings*

Note: Punch may also be served in punch bowl if desired.

Belgian Wassail

2 oranges

2 lemons

4 cups water

1 tablespoon allspice

2 cinnamon sticks

1 cup sugar

1 gallon MOTT'S® Apple Juice

In large bowl, squeeze juice from oranges and lemons. Reserve the juice and rinds. In large saucepan boil water, orange and lemon rinds, allspice and cinnamon. Simmer 1 hour. Remove rinds and add sugar, apple juice and reserved juice. Stir to dissolve sugar. Serve hot.   *Makes 20 servings*

Mocha Nog

Prep and Cook Time: 10 minutes

1 quart eggnog

1 tablespoon instant French vanilla or regular coffee granules

¼ cup coffee-flavored liqueur

1. Heat eggnog and coffee granules in large saucepan over medium heat until mixture is hot and coffee granules are dissolved; do not boil. Remove from heat; stir in coffee liqueur.

2. Pour eggnog into individual mugs. *Makes 8 servings*

Cranberry Sangría

1 bottle (750 ml) Beaujolais or dry red wine

1 cup cranberry juice cocktail

1 cup orange juice

½ cup cranberry-flavored liqueur (optional)

1 orange,* thinly sliced

1 lime,* thinly sliced

The orange and lime may be scored before slicing to add a special touch. To score, make a lengthwise groove in the fruit with a citrus stripper. Continue to make grooves ¼ to ½ inch apart until the entire fruit has been grooved.

Combine wine, cranberry juice cocktail, orange juice, liqueur, orange slices and lime slices in large glass pitcher. Chill 2 to 8 hours before serving.

Pour into glasses; add orange and/or lime slices from sangría to each glass. *Makes about 7 cups, 10 to 12 servings*

Sparkling Sangría: Just before serving, tilt pitcher and slowly add 2 cups well-chilled sparkling water or club soda. Pour into glasses; add orange and/or lime slices from sangría to each glass. Makes about 9 cups, or 12 to 15 servings.

Mocha Nog

Mulled Wine

2 bottles (750 ml each)
   dry red wine, such as
   Cabernet Sauvignon

1 cup light corn syrup

1 cup water

1 square (8 inches) double-
   thickness cheesecloth

   Peel of 1 large orange

1 cinnamon stick, broken
   into halves

8 whole cloves

1 whole nutmeg

SLOW COOKER DIRECTIONS

Combine wine, corn syrup and water in slow cooker. Rinse cheesecloth; squeeze out water. Wrap orange peel, cinnamon stick halves, cloves and nutmeg in cheesecloth. Tie securely with cotton string or strip of cheesecloth. Add to slow cooker. Cover and cook on HIGH 2 to 2½ hours. Discard spice bag; ladle wine into mugs.

Makes 12 servings

Hot Spiced Cider

Prep Time: 20 minutes

2 quarts apple cider

⅔ cup KARO® Light or Dark
   Corn Syrup

3 cinnamon sticks

½ teaspoon whole cloves

1 lemon, sliced

   Cinnamon sticks and lemon
   slices (optional)

1. In medium saucepan combine cider, corn syrup, cinnamon sticks, cloves and lemon slices.

2. Bring to boil over medium-high heat. Reduce heat; simmer 15 minutes. Remove spices.

3. If desired, garnish each serving with a cinnamon stick and lemon slice.

Makes about 10 servings

Mulled Wine

Happy Hour

Honey Orange Marys

4 cups tomato juice

½ cup orange juice

¼ cup honey

2 teaspoons prepared
   horseradish

½ teaspoon celery salt

Hot pepper sauce to taste

Worcestershire sauce to
   taste

Pepper to taste

Ice cubes

Celery sticks (optional)

Combine tomato juice, orange juice, honey, horseradish and celery salt in large pitcher; stir until well blended. Season to taste with hot pepper sauce, Worcestershire sauce and black pepper. Serve over ice in tall glasses. Garnish with celery sticks, if desired.

Makes about 5 cups

Favorite recipe from **National Honey Board**

Top to bottom: Passion Potion (page 368) and Honey Orange Mary

Sour Apple Margarita

3 ounces MR & MRS T®
Margarita Mix

1 ounce sour apple liqueur

1½ ounces tequila

½ ounce ROSE'S® Lime Juice

½ ounce ROSE'S® Triple Sec

½ cup ice

1 lime, sliced

50/50 cinnamon/sugar
mixture (optional)

Mix first 6 ingredients in shaker. Shake well. Coat rim of martini glass with lime and dip in cinnamon/sugar mixture, if desired. Strain into glass and serve.

Makes 1 serving

Fresh Fruit Lemonade

1 to 1½ cups sliced ripe
strawberries, or whole
raspberries or
blueberries

Juice of 6 SUNKIST® lemons
(1 cup)

1 cup sugar

4 cups cold water

1 fresh lemon, unpeeled, cut
in cartwheel slices

Ice cubes

In blender or food processor, combine berries, lemon juice and sugar; blend until smooth. Pour into large pitcher. Add cold water, lemon cartwheel slices and ice; stir well. Garnish each serving with additional fruit and/or fresh mint leaves, if desired.

Makes about 6 (8-ounce) servings

*Sour Apple Margarita and
Piquant Veracruz Clams (page 306)*

Snowbird Mocktails

Prep time: 10 minutes

3 cups pineapple juice

1 can (14 ounces) sweetened condensed milk

1 can (6 ounces) frozen orange juice concentrate, thawed

½ teaspoon coconut extract

1 bottle (32 ounces) ginger ale, chilled

1. Combine pineapple juice, sweetened condensed milk, orange juice concentrate and coconut extract in large pitcher; stir well. Refrigerate, covered, up to 1 week.

2. To serve, pour ½ cup pineapple juice mixture into individual glasses (over crushed ice, if desired). Top off each glass with about ⅓ cup ginger ale. *Makes 10 servings*

Tip: Store unopened cans of sweetened condensed milk at room temperature up to 6 months. Once opened, store in airtight container in refrigerator for up to 5 days.

Peaches and Cream Punch

4 cups boiling water

6 LIPTON® Brisk Regular or Decaffeinated Tea Bags

4 cans (12 ounces each) peach nectar, chilled

2 cups Champagne or seltzer, chilled

1 container (16 ounces) frozen vanilla lowfat yogurt

In teapot, pour boiling water over tea bags; cover and brew 5 minutes. Remove tea bags and cool.

In chilled 4-quart punch bowl, blend peach nectar with tea. Just before serving, add Champagne. Top with scoops of yogurt and garnish, if desired, with fresh peach slices. Serve immediately.

Makes 24 (4-ounce) servings

Sparkling White Sangria

Prep Time: 15 minutes, plus standing and chilling

1 cup KARO® Light Corn Syrup

1 orange, sliced

1 lemon, sliced

1 lime, sliced

½ cup orange-flavored liqueur

1 bottle (750 ml) dry white wine

2 tablespoons lemon juice

1 bottle (12 ounces) club soda or seltzer, chilled

Additional fresh fruit (optional)

1. In large pitcher combine corn syrup, orange, lemon and lime slices and liqueur. Let stand 20 to 30 minutes, stirring occasionally.

2. Stir in wine and lemon juice. Refrigerate.

3. Just before serving, add soda and ice cubes. If desired, garnish with additional fruit. *Makes about 6 (8-ounce) servings*

Pepperita

1¼ ounces gold tequila

⅔ ounce Grand Marnier

Juice of half a lime

½ teaspoon TABASCO® brand Green Pepper Sauce

Lime slice for garnish

Rub rim of glass with cut side of lime, then dip rim into saucer of salt. Fill glass with ice. Pour first three ingredients into ice-filled cocktail shaker or pitcher and shake or stir vigorously. Strain into ice-filled glass. Shake in TABASCO® Green Pepper Sauce and stir. Garnish with lime slice. *Makes 1 serving*

Tip: Use margarita or sweet and sour mix to make drink as directed on label. Shake in ½ to 1 teaspoon TABASCO® Green Pepper Sauce per drink and stir.

Toasted Coco Colada

3 ounces MR & MRS T®
Piña Colada Mix

1½ ounces coconut rum

½ ounce caramel syrup

½ ounce coconut syrup

1 cup ice

1 lime wedge

Toasted coconut flakes,
ground (as needed)

Blend first 5 ingredients in blender until slushy. Coat rim of daiquiri glass with lime wedge; dip glass into ground toasted coconut flakes. Pour into daiquiri glass. *Makes 1 drink*

Nectarine Sunrise

4 fresh California nectarines

1 can (6 ounces) frozen
limeade concentrate

⅔ cup tequila

2 to 3 cups crushed ice

½ cup grenadine syrup

Fresh mint sprigs

Slice 1 nectarine; set aside for garnish. Coarsely chop remaining nectarines. In blender, combine chopped nectarines, limeade and tequila; purée until smooth. Gradually add crushed ice, blending until slushy and mixture measures 5 cups. Place 1 tablespoon grenadine syrup in each of 8 stemmed glasses. Add nectarine mixture. Top each with mint sprig and nectarine slice on side of glass. Serve immediately. *Makes 8 servings*

Favorite recipe from **California Tree Fruit Agreement**

Merry Mango Fizz

1 bottle (64 ounces) MAUNA LA'I® ¡Mango Mango!® Juice Drink

1 bottle (32 ounces) cranberry juice cocktail

1 bottle (32 ounces) ginger ale

2 cups vanilla ice cream

Fresh or frozen strawberries, as needed

Combine Mauna La'i ¡Mango Mango! Juice Drink and cranberry juice cocktail in large punch bowl. Fifteen minutes before serving, add ginger ale and ice cream. Do not stir. Garnish with strawberries.

Makes 24 servings

Bloody Mary Mix

1 quart vegetable juice cocktail

2 tablespoons HEINZ® Worcestershire Sauce

1 tablespoon fresh lime or lemon juice

¼ teaspoon granulated sugar

¼ teaspoon pepper

¼ teaspoon hot pepper sauce

⅛ teaspoon garlic powder

In pitcher, thoroughly combine vegetable juice, Worcestershire sauce, lime juice, sugar, pepper, hot pepper sauce and garlic powder; cover and chill. Serve over ice. Garnish with celery stalks and lime wedges, if desired.

Makes about 1 quart

Note: To prepare Bloody Mary Cocktail, add 3 or 4 parts Bloody Mary Mix to 1 part vodka.

Left to right: Merry Mango Fizz, Mocha Colada (page 360) and Toasted Coco Colada (page 357)

Mocha Colada

3 ounces MR & MRS T® Piña
Colada Mix

1 ounce COCO CASA® Cream
of Coconut

2 ounces cold espresso (or
other strong coffee)

1 cup ice

½ tablespoon chocolate syrup

Chocolate covered espresso
bean, for garnish

Blend first 4 ingredients in blender until slushy. Pour into tall glass and garnish with chocolate syrup and espresso bean.

Makes 1 serving

Celebration Punch

1 can (46 fluid ounces) DEL
MONTE® Pineapple Juice,
chilled

1 can (46 fluid ounces)
apricot nectar, chilled

1 cup orange juice

¼ cup fresh lime juice

2 tablespoons grenadine

1 cup rum (optional)

Ice cubes

1. Combine all ingredients in punch bowl.

2. Garnish with pineapple wedges and lime slices, if desired.

Makes 16 (6-ounce) servings

Sangria Blush

1 cup orange juice

½ cup sugar

1 bottle (1.5 liters) white zinfandel wine

¼ cup lime or lemon juice

1 orange, thinly sliced and seeded

1 lime, thinly sliced and seeded

16 to 20 ice cubes

Combine orange juice and sugar in small pan. Cook over medium heat, stirring occasionally, until sugar is dissolved. Pour into 2-quart container with tight-fitting lid. Add wine, lime juice and sliced fruits. Cover; refrigerate 2 hours for flavors to blend. Place ice cubes in small punch bowl or large pitcher. Pour wine mixture over ice.

Makes 8 servings

Honey Lemonade with Frozen Fruit Cubes

1½ cups lemon juice

¾ cup honey

9 cups water

48 small pieces assorted fruit

Combine lemon juice and honey in large pitcher; stir until honey is dissolved. Stir in water. Place 1 to 2 pieces of fruit in each compartment of 2 ice cube trays. Fill each compartment with honey lemonade and freeze until firm. Chill remaining lemonade. To serve, divide frozen fruit cubes between tall glasses and fill with remaining lemonade.

Makes 9 cups

*Favorite recipe from **National Honey Board***

Daiquiri

¾ cup MAUNA LA'I® ¡Mango Mango!® Juice Drink

3 tablespoons rum

1 tablespoon ROSE'S® Lime Juice

1 teaspoon sugar

Ice, as needed

Combine Mauna La'i ¡Mango Mango! Juice Drink, rum, lime juice and sugar in shaker with ice. Pour into tall glass filled with ice.

Makes 1 drink

Mango Margarita

½ cup MAUNA LA'I® ¡Mango Mango!® Juice Drink

1 ounce tequila

Dash ROSE'S® Triple Sec

Dash ROSE'S® Lime Juice

Lime wedge, as needed

Ice, as needed

Combine Mauna La'i ¡Mango Mango! Juice Drink, tequila, triple sec and lime juice in shaker with ice. Pour into salt-rimmed margarita glass. Garnish with lime.

Makes 1 drink

Clockwise from top: Mango Margarita, Kiwi Magarita (page 370) and Daiquiri

Piña Colada Punch

3 cups water

10 whole cloves

4 cardamom pods

2 sticks cinnamon

1 can (12 ounces) frozen pineapple juice concentrate, thawed

1 pint low-fat piña colada frozen yogurt, softened*

1¼ cups lemon seltzer water

1¼ teaspoons rum extract

¾ teaspoon coconut extract (optional)

*You may substitute pineapple sherbet for low-fat piña colada frozen yogurt. When using pineapple sherbet, use the coconut extract for a more authentic flavor.

1. Combine water, cloves, cardamom and cinnamon in small saucepan. Bring to a boil over high heat; reduce heat to low. Simmer, covered, 5 minutes; cool. Strain and discard spices.

2. Combine spiced water, pineapple juice concentrate and frozen yogurt in small punch bowl or pitcher. Stir until frozen yogurt is melted. Stir in seltzer water, rum extract and coconut extract, if desired. Garnish with mint sprigs, if desired.

Makes 12 (4-ounce) servings

Dole® Juice Spritzer

Prep Time: 5 minutes

½ cup DOLE® Country Raspberry Juice or Pineapple Juice

½ cup mineral or sparkling water

• Pour juice and mineral water over ice cubes in large glass. Garnish with lime wedge and citrus curl, if desired. *Makes 1 serving*

Piña Colada Punch

Hot Spiced Toddy

1 cup MAUNA LA'I® ¡Mango Mango!® Juice Drink

Dash ground cinnamon

⅛ cup dark rum (optional)

1 tablespoon brown sugar

2 teaspoons butter (optional)

1 cinnamon stick

Heat Mauna La'i ¡Mango Mango! Juice Drink and cinnamon in small saucepan. Add rum, brown sugar, and butter in mug. Pour hot juice drink into mug and stir gently. Garnish with cinnamon stick.

Makes 1 serving

Festive Fruit Punch

3 cups water

⅔ cup sugar

20 whole cloves

2 sticks cinnamon

4 to 6 pieces candied ginger

1 bottle (40 ounces) white grape juice, chilled

1 bottle (32 ounces) raspberry or boysenberry fruit juice blend (with apple juice), chilled

Juice of 6 SUNKIST® lemons (1 cup)

In saucepan, combine water, sugar and spices. Bring to boil, stirring until sugar dissolves. Reduce heat; simmer 5 minutes. Chill; remove spices. To serve, in punch bowl combine all ingredients. For garnish, float lemon cartwheel slices in punch, if desired.

Makes about 13 cups (eighteen 6-ounce servings)

Sangrita

Prep Time: 3 minutes

3 cups DEL MONTE® Tomato
   Juice

1½ cups orange juice

½ cup salsa

   Juice of 1 medium lime

1. Mix all ingredients in large pitcher; chill.

2. Serve over ice with fruit garnishes, if desired.

Makes 6 (6-ounce) servings

Margaritas, Albuquerque Style

1 lime, cut into wedges

   Coarse salt

1 can (6 ounces) frozen lime
   concentrate

¾ cup tequila

6 tablespoons Triple Sec

1 can (12 ounces) lemon-lime
   or grapefruit soda

3 to 4 cups ice cubes

   Lime twist for garnish

   Lime peel for garnish

Rub rim of each cocktail glass with lime wedge; swirl glass in salt to coat rim. Combine half of each of the remaining ingredients, except garnishes, in blender container; blend until ice is finely chopped and mixture is slushy. Pour into salt-rimmed glasses. Repeat with remaining ingredients. Garnish, if desired. *Makes 7 to 8 servings*

Champagne Punch

1 orange

1 lemon

¼ cup cranberry-flavored liqueur or cognac

¼ cup orange-flavored liqueur or Triple Sec

1 bottle (750 ml) pink or regular champagne or sparkling white wine, well chilled

Fresh cranberries (optional)

Citrus strips for garnish

Remove colored peel, not white pith, from orange and lemon in long thin strips with citrus peeler. Refrigerate orange and lemon for another use. Combine peels and cranberry- and orange-flavored liqueurs in glass pitcher. Cover and refrigerate 2 to 6 hours.

Just before serving, tilt pitcher to one side and slowly pour in champagne. Leave peels in pitcher for added flavor. Place a cranberry in bottom of each glass. Pour into champagne glasses. Garnish with citrus strips tied in knots, if desired.

Makes 4 cups (6 to 8 servings)

Nonalchoholic Cranberry Punch: Pour 3 cups well-chilled club soda into ⅔ cup (6 ounces) cranberry cocktail concentrate, thawed. Makes 3½ cups (6 servings).

Passion Potion

1½ cups pink grapefruit juice, chilled

3 tablespoons honey

Ice cubes

¼ cup rum or vodka*

*If desired, omit rum or vodka and top each glass with ¼ cup club soda.

Combine grapefruit juice and honey in pitcher; stir until honey is dissolved. Fill two 12-ounce glasses with ice. Pour 2 tablespoons rum over ice in each glass and add grapefruit juice mixture.

Makes 2 cups

Favorite recipe from **National Honey Board**

Champagne Punch

Kiwi Margarita

3½ ounces MR & MRS T®
    Margarita Mix

2 ripe kiwi, peeled

1 cup strawberry sorbet

1½ ounces white rum

2 ounces club soda

1 lime, sliced

    MR & MRS T® Margarita
    Salt (optional)

Blend first 5 ingredients in blender on low speed until smooth.*
Coat rim of glass with lime and dip in margarita salt, if desired.
Pour into glass. *Makes 1 serving*

Be careful not to blend too long as crushed kiwi seeds taste bitter.

Hot Cranberry-Lemon Wine Punch

3 cups water

¾ to 1 cup sugar

20 whole cloves

2 sticks cinnamon

1 bottle (750 ml) rosé wine

1 bottle (32 ounces)
    cranberry juice cocktail

Juice of 6 SUNKIST® lemons
    (1 cup)

In saucepot, combine water, sugar and spices. Bring to boil, stirring
until sugar dissolves. Reduce heat; simmer 5 minutes. Remove
spices. Add remaining ingredients; heat. For garnish, float clove-
studded lemon cartwheel slices in punch, if desired.

Makes about 11 cups (eighteen 5-ounce servings)

Cold Cranberry-Lemon Wine Punch: After simmering water,
sugar and spices, chill syrup mixture. To serve, in punch bowl
combine all ingredients. Add ½ cup brandy, if desired. Add ice
or float an ice ring.

Bloody Bull

Prep Time: 5 minutes   **Chill Time:** 30 minutes

3 cups tomato juice

2 cans (10½ ounces each) condensed beef broth

1 cup vodka (optional)

3 tablespoons *Frank's® RedHot®* Cayenne Pepper Sauce

2 tablespoons *French's®* Worcestershire Sauce

2 tablespoons prepared horseradish

1 tablespoon lemon juice

Combine all ingredients in large pitcher; refrigerate. Serve over ice.

Makes 6 servings

Sangria Tea Sparkler

3 cups brewed LIPTON® Regular or Decaffeinated Tea, chilled

2 cups chilled grape juice

⅓ cup sugar

1 medium orange, sliced

1 medium lemon, sliced

1 medium lime, sliced

Few drops angostura bitters (optional)

Chilled club soda

In large pitcher, combine all ingredients except club soda; chill at least 2 hours. Just before serving, add a splash of soda. Pour into ice-filled glasses and garnish, if desired, with additional orange, lemon and lime slices.

Makes 5 servings

Citrus Cooler

2 cups fresh squeezed
   orange juice
2 cups unsweetened
   pineapple juice
1 teaspoon fresh lemon juice
¾ teaspoon vanilla extract
¾ teaspoon coconut extract
2 cups cold sparkling water

Combine juices and extracts in large pitcher; refrigerate until cold. Stir in sparkling water; serve over ice. *Makes 8 servings*

White Sangria

1 carton (64 ounces) DOLE®
   Pineapple Orange
   Banana Juice
2 cups fruity white wine
2 cups sliced DOLE® Fresh
   Strawberries
1 orange, thinly sliced
1 lime, thinly sliced
¼ cup sugar
¼ cup orange-flavored liqueur
   Ice cubes
   Mint sprigs for garnish

• Combine juice, wine, strawberries, orange, lime, sugar, and liqueur in 2 large pitchers; cover and refrigerate 2 hours to blend flavors. Serve over ice. Garnish with mint sprigs. *Makes 20 servings*

Citrus Cooler

Acknowledgments

The publishers would like to thank the companies and organizations listed below for the use of their recipes and photographs in this publication.

A.1.® Steak Sauce
Birds Eye®
Bob Evans®
Butterball® Turkey Company
California Tree Fruit Agreement
Cherry Marketing Institute
Colorado Potato Administrative Committee
ConAgra Grocery Products Company
Del Monte Corporation
Dole Food Company, Inc.
Fleischmann's® Original Spread
Florida Department of Agriculture and Consumer Services, Bureau of Seafood and Aquaculture
Grey Poupon® Dijon Mustard
Guiltless Gourmet®
Hebrew National®
Heinz U.S.A.
Hershey Foods Corporation
Hillshire Farm®
The HV Company
Kikkoman International Inc.
The Kingsford Products Company
Kraft Foods Holdings

Lawry's® Foods, Inc.
Mauna La'i® is a registered trademark of Mott's, Inc.
McIlhenny Company (TABASCO® brand Pepper Sauce)
Holland House® is a registered trademark of Mott's, Inc.
Mott's® is a registered trademark of Mott's, Inc.
Nabisco Biscuit and Snack Divison
National Fisheries Institute
National Honey Board
National Pork Board
National Turkey Federation
Nestlé USA
Reckitt Benckiser
The J.M. Smucker Company
StarKist® Seafood Company
Sun•Maid® Growers of California
Sunkist Growers
Uncle Ben's Inc.
Unilever Bestfoods North America
Veg-All®
Wisconsin Milk Marketing Board

Index

Index

Index

Index

Index

Index

Index

Index

Index

METRIC CONVERSION CHART

VOLUME MEASUREMENTS (dry)

1/8 teaspoon = 0.5 mL
1/4 teaspoon = 1 mL
1/2 teaspoon = 2 mL
3/4 teaspoon = 4 mL
1 teaspoon = 5 mL
1 tablespoon = 15 mL
2 tablespoons = 30 mL
1/4 cup = 60 mL
1/3 cup = 75 mL
1/2 cup = 125 mL
2/3 cup = 150 mL
3/4 cup = 175 mL
1 cup = 250 mL
2 cups = 1 pint = 500 mL
3 cups = 750 mL
4 cups = 1 quart = 1 L

VOLUME MEASUREMENTS (fluid)

1 fluid ounce (2 tablespoons) = 30 mL
4 fluid ounces (1/2 cup) = 125 mL
8 fluid ounces (1 cup) = 250 mL
12 fluid ounces (1 1/2 cups) = 375 mL
16 fluid ounces (2 cups) = 500 mL

WEIGHTS (mass)

1/2 ounce = 15 g
1 ounce = 30 g
3 ounces = 90 g
4 ounces = 120 g
8 ounces = 225 g
10 ounces = 285 g
12 ounces = 360 g
16 ounces = 1 pound = 450 g

DIMENSIONS

1/16 inch = 2 mm
1/8 inch = 3 mm
1/4 inch = 6 mm
1/2 inch = 1.5 cm
3/4 inch = 2 cm
1 inch = 2.5 cm

OVEN TEMPERATURES

250°F = 120°C
275°F = 140°C
300°F = 150°C
325°F = 160°C
350°F = 180°C
375°F = 190°C
400°F = 200°C
425°F = 220°C
450°F = 230°C

BAKING PAN SIZES

Utensil	Size in Inches/Quarts	Metric Volume	Size in Centimeters
Baking or	8×8×2	2 L	20×20×5
Cake Pan	9×9×2	2.5 L	23×23×5
(square or	12×8×2	3 L	30×20×5
rectangular)	13×9×2	3.5 L	33×23×5
Loaf Pan	8×4×3	1.5 L	20×10×7
	9×5×3	2 L	23×13×7
Round Layer	8×1½	1.2 L	20×4
Cake Pan	9×1½	1.5 L	23×4
Pie Plate	8×1¼	750 mL	20×3
	9×1¼	1 L	23×3
Baking Dish	1 quart	1 L	—
or Casserole	1½ quart	1.5 L	—
	2 quart	2 L	—